Don't Go Broke in Retirement

A Simple Plan to Build Lifetime Retirement Income

Praise for *Don't Go Broke in Retirement*

"When you retire, or are planning to retire, there's just one thing you need to know: Can you make your savings last as long as *you* will? Steve Vernon helps you answer that question—putting you on track to financial security for life."

— **Jane Bryant Quinn**, author of *How to Make Your Money Last: The Indispensable Retirement Guide*

"This is exactly what every pre-retiree needs—a simple framework for planning and maximizing your retirement income, within a structure that takes away much of the financial worry so you can relax and enjoy this next stage of life."

— **Terry Savage**, author of *The Savage Truth on Money* and a nationally syndicated financial columnist

"Retirement shouldn't be about fiddling with spreadsheets or staying glued to CNBC. *Don't Go Broke in Retirement* teaches how to construct a solid financial plan for retirement in a straightforward, easy-to-implement way. This elegant volume gets right to the point so retirees can get on with their lives."

— **Christine Benz**, director of personal finance and a senior columnist for Morningstar Inc.

"Steve Vernon's *Don't Go Broke in Retirement* is a well-written, smart book that really does offer a simple plan for building lifetime retirement income. The examples and key takeaways are based on a sound strategy and given with common sense to reinforce the average person's own experience plus help them achieve security and success by not going broke. Vernon's expertise, coupled with practical suggestions, provides real solutions."

— **M. Cindy Hounsell**, president of the Women's Institute for a Secure Retirement (WISER)

Praise for *Don't Go Broke in Retirement*

"Whether in life or with one's finances, simple solutions are almost always superior. In his new book, Steve Vernon explains with brilliant simplicity how to worry less about money and enjoy life more."

— **Allan Roth**, AARP *Money* contributor and author of *How a Second Grader Beats Wall Street*

"Some of the most important decisions that middle-income families must make are when to retire, when to claim Social Security, and how to use their savings in retirement. *Don't Go Broke in Retirement* offers a practical, straightforward approach to setting up a retirement income plan tailored to the needs of typical middle-income Americans."

— **Anna M. Rappaport**, FSA, MAAA, past president of the Society of Actuaries, internationally known retirement expert, and a phased retiree

"The most complicated financial decision folks have to make regarding their retirement security is made easy by Steve Vernon. An easy read that's empowering through easy-to-understand financial decision-making processes for all near retirees, financial experts, and retirement plan sponsors thinking about retirement income for their 401(k) plan."

— **Robert Melia**, executive director of the Institutional Retirement Income Council

"This valuable volume explains how middle-income households can make their retirement savings last the rest of their lives. It's written in clear English by a real expert, and the approach is simple. Buy the book, read it, and enjoy the security of knowing you won't go broke in retirement."

— **Alicia Munnell**, Peter F. Drucker Professor of Management Sciences and director of the Center for Retirement Research, Boston College

Praise for *Don't Go Broke in Retirement*

"*Don't Go Broke in Retirement* explains, in plain English, the complex decisions needed for a secure retirement, and it's written in a practical, implementable way. I think it will really help people."

— **Fred Reish**, partner and leader, Financial Services ERISA Practice Team, Faegre Drinker, member of the Certified Financial Planner Board Public Policy Council

"Steve Vernon has a gift for sorting through the clutter on retirement advice and focusing on the things that matter most. *Don't Go Broke in Retirement* is must reading if you're trying to decide when to retire and how you'll replace your paycheck after you quit work."

— **Mark Miller**, retirement journalist, author, and podcaster

"Steve Vernon does a masterful job explaining a simple approach toward building a retirement income plan that anyone can master. Despite the simplicity, his approach is actually very close to how academics solve the retirement problem using more sophisticated theory: Build a base of lifetime income that you cannot outlive to cover your basics and then supplement this with additional spending from what remains. Job well done."

— **Wade D. Pfau**, PhD, CFA, RICP, director of the Retirement Income Certified Professional program at The American College of Financial Services and founder of RetirementResearcher.com

"For most middle-class American workers, the ability to earn a paycheck is their most important "asset." However, many, perhaps most, are unprepared for decision-making as they transition into and throughout retirement. Steve Vernon's guidance may help you minimize the chances you'll experience 'buyer's remorse' with respect to your retirement income decision-making."

— **Jack Towarnicky**, researcher for the American Retirement Association and past executive director of the Plan Sponsor Council of America

Don't Go Broke in Retirement

A Simple Plan to Build Lifetime Retirement Income

STEVE VERNON, FSA

 *Rest-of-Life* Communications
Oxnard, California

For more information:
Rest-of-Life Communications: www.restoflife.com

Project management: Markman Editorial Services, www.MarlaMarkman.com

Book cover and design: Lisa Winger, WinBach Marketing Images, www.winbach.com

Library of Congress Cataloging-in-Publication Data:
Vernon, Steven G., 1953-, author.

Don't go broke in retirement: a simple plan to build lifetime retirement income

Includes bibliographical references and index. | Oxnard, CA: Rest-of-Life Communications, 2020.

ISBN: 978-0-9853846-6-1 | LCCN: 2020902517

LCSH Retirement–United States–Planning. | Retirement income–United States–Planning. | Investments–United States. | Retirees–United States–Finance. | Social Security–United States. | 401(k)–United States.

BISAC BUSINESS & ECONOMICS / Personal Finance / Retirement Planning

LCC HQ1063.2.U6 .V47 2020 | DDC 646.7/93--dc23

ISBN: 978-0-9853846-6-1 (Print)
ISBN: 978-0-9853846-7-8 (e-Readers)

TO MELINDA

My wife and sweetie,
who provided tremendous help and encouragement

ALSO BY STEVE VERNON

*Retirement Game-Changers: Strategies for a Healthy,
Financially Secure, and Fulfilling Long Life*

*Money for Life: Turn Your IRA and 401(k) Into
a Lifetime Retirement Paycheck*

*Recession-Proof Your Retirement Years:
Simple Retirement Planning Strategies That Work
Through Thick or Thin*

*The Quest: For Long Life, Health and Prosperity
(DVD/workbook set)*

*Live Long and Prosper!
Invest in Your Happiness, Health and Wealth for
Retirement and Beyond*

*Don't Work Forever! Simple Steps Baby Boomers
Must Take to Ever Retire*

For bulk purchases of *Don't Go Broke in Retirement*, *Retirement Game-Changers*, *Money for Life*, *Recession-Proof Your Retirement Years*, or *The Quest* DVD, please email steve.vernon@restoflife.com.

TABLE OF CONTENTS

Introduction

Are you worried about making your retirement savings last the rest of your life? Are you unsure about how much you can spend on living expenses throughout your retirement without using up your savings too quickly? Are you nervous about stock market crashes that could derail your retirement in future years?

If any of these questions have been keeping you up at night, you're not alone. Millions of older workers are approaching their retirement years, and they're anxiously mulling over these tough questions.

Fortunately, if you're even a little concerned about outliving your money in retirement, then you've come to the right place! This book outlines a retirement income strategy that helps you survive the economic turmoil that's inevitable during a long retirement, so you can sleep better at night.

The *Spend Safely in Retirement Strategy* helps you make critical decisions

As you approach retirement, there are five essential decisions you'll need to make:

- When to retire
- Whether to work part time for a few years after leaving your full-time job

- When to start your Social Security benefits
- How to deploy your savings in retirement
- How to protect your retirement income from financial crises

All of these decisions can be confusing and intimidating for many people. If you have an effective plan, however, you'll probably feel more confident about your retirement years.

To help you build a retirement income plan that works throughout your retirement years, this book introduces you to the *Spend Safely in Retirement Strategy* (or, for brevity's sake, the *Spend Safely Strategy*). It's a straightforward and effective way to make key retirement decisions without getting help from a financial adviser. Of course, if you feel better working with a planner, then the information in this book can help you have a more informed conversation with a trusted adviser.

But let's go back a step: Why do so many workers these days need help planning for a financially secure retirement? The fact is, times have changed and most older workers no longer participate in a traditional pension plan, which would pay you a monthly income for the rest of your life, no matter how long you live. These valuable plans helped millions of workers in previous generations retire with comfort and security.

Today, however, to fund their retirement, many workers depend primarily on Social Security and substantial savings they've built up in an IRA, 401(k) plan, or other retirement savings plan, such as a SEP-IRA, SIMPLE IRA, 403(b) plan for employees of nonprofit employers, or 457 plan for government employees. But most of these plans don't have straightforward options for converting your hard-earned savings into a stream of retirement income. As a result, you're on your own to make these critical decisions. The *Spend Safely Strategy* shows you how to generate lifetime retirement income using investment funds that are typically available in the retirement savings plans mentioned above.

The *Spend Safely Strategy* is a *baseline* retirement income strategy that's easy to understand and feasible to implement in most retirement savings programs. To help you even further, this book also describes straightforward adjustments you can make to personalize the baseline strategy to meet your own personal goals and circumstances. For example, you could decide to increase the amount of income that's protected from financial risks, if that would make you feel more secure.

This book can also help you make other tough retirement choices. For instance, once you understand how much retirement income you can expect to receive both from Social Security and by deploying your savings, you'll need to decide how long you should continue to work full time, whether you should consider working part time, and how much money you can afford to spend on living expenses in retirement. All of these choices could reflect the hard realities of your circumstances.

With that in mind, note that the subtitle of this book doesn't promise an *easy* plan to build retirement income. Instead, the effective solutions I've described in *Don't Go Broke in Retirement* should be *simple* for you to understand and apply if you take the time to read through this book and digest the main ideas. Then you can apply your common sense to these potentially tough choices.

A few important caveats

I've intentionally kept this book short so you're not overwhelmed with too much information. To do that, I describe just one straightforward, effective approach to making retirement decisions and generating streams of retirement income. This one approach should be both simple to understand and reasonable to implement.

And while there are certainly other methods for generating retirement income, many are much more complex. Other options might be appropriate for you if you've saved well over $1 million or if you have personal goals that can't be addressed by the straightforward refinements in this book. In such cases, this book can still be useful for you because it can help you determine whether more complex strategies—compared to the baseline *Spend Safely Strategy*—can better meet your needs.

What isn't covered

Another thing to keep in mind: In addition to determining how to deploy your retirement savings to generate a lifetime retirement income, there are other key decisions you'll need to make and other tasks you'll need to complete as you transition into retirement. These decisions and tasks include:

- taking inventory of your assets, debts, and living expenses,
- finding work in retirement if you need it,
- protecting against the potentially high cost of medical and long-term care,

- deciding where to live in retirement,
- maintaining your health, and
- determining what you'll do with your new freedom.

To keep this short book focused on the key task of generating retirement income, however, I don't cover these other decisions here. If you're interested in learning more about these decisions and potential strategies, please see my recent book, *Retirement Game-Changers: Strategies for a Healthy, Financially Secure, and Fulfilling Long Life.*

About me

So who am I and why did I write this book? For more than 30 years, I worked as a consulting actuary, helping large employers design and manage their retirement plans. I was on the front lines of the transition from traditional pension plans to 401(k) plans that took place during the 1980s, 1990s and early 2000s. During this transition, employers placed the responsibility for investing and managing retirement savings to last for life squarely on the shoulders of their workers and retirees.

And that change led to my encore career. Since 2006, my life's work has been to help individuals and society cope with the new retirement planning responsibilities we now face, especially given the fact that millions of Americans are living long lives and need to have strategies in place to help keep them financially secure for all those years.

I also write books and online columns about retirement strategies, and I deliver retirement planning workshops.

Meeting face-to-face with people who are struggling with the challenges of retirement planning in the 21st century better informs my work at the Stanford Center on Longevity (SCL), where I work as a research scholar to help develop strategies people can use to fund a long life. In fact, the insights and strategies I've outlined in this book are based on recent SCL research I've been involved with and published. The reports based on this research are listed in the "Helpful Resources" section at the back of this book.

One thing I've never done, at any time in my career, is to sell financial products or insurance. I want to help you without being influenced by how I get paid.

It's worth your time to do the job right

Back to the task at hand: It will take several hours of reading for you to understand the income-generating strategy and refinements described in this book, and also to learn how to implement this strategy to best meet your needs. But I think you'll discover the time is worth it: You're planning for your financial security for the *rest of your life*, which could last 30 years or more. To do a good job, you need to think long term. So it's well worth putting in some time *now* to develop solid plans for the future—plans that should help put your mind at ease about being financially secure no matter how long you live.

In fact, feedback I've received from attendees of my retirement planning workshops and readers of my columns and books confirms my belief that it's worth your time to carefully build a portfolio of risk-protected retirement income. For these people, the financial crisis of 2020 caused by the COVID-19 pandemic gave them an opportunity to stress-test the *Spend Safely Strategy*, and it came through with flying colors, according to the emails I've received.

After digging into this book, I hope you'll begin to feel excited about the fun and fulfilling experiences lying ahead in your retirement years, instead of feeling stressed about money.

If you're ready, let's get started!

The Basics

In this section, you'll learn the main ideas of the *Spend Safely in Retirement Strategy* in four short chapters. If you understand and implement the concepts in just these chapters, you'll be well on your way to living a financially secure life. You'll be able to enjoy a retirement income that will last for the rest of your life, no matter how long you live, and no matter what happens in the stock market.

Chapter 1

Introducing the *Spend Safely in Retirement Strategy*

Deciding when you can afford to retire and then determining how to deploy your savings to generate retirement income for the rest of your life can be both confusing and intimidating. But it doesn't need to be this way.

Since the subtitle of this book promises a simple plan to build retirement income, I'm going to keep things simple by introducing the overall three-step plan in this first chapter. Once you're familiar with these steps, I'll then cover the details in subsequent chapters.

First, though, let's examine an essential idea about your retirement savings.

Don't spend your retirement savings!

That's right, you heard me, though let me qualify that statement a bit: Don't spend your retirement savings on your living expenses in retirement.

Instead, use your savings to generate retirement income

that lasts the rest of your life, and spend just the income that your savings generates. This way, you won't run out of money during your lifetime, no matter how long you live.

Let me tell you why it's best to use your savings as a Retirement Income Generator, or RIG for short. When left to their own devices, people tend to fall into one of two camps:

Camp #1: These are the people who are extremely worried about outliving their money. They tend to hoard their savings for that proverbial "rainy day" and try to withdraw as little as possible from their savings. Many people in this camp pass away with a lot of money in the bank—money they could have spent while they were alive.

Camp #2: These are the people who use their retirement savings like a checking account to pay for their living expenses as they come due, or for special extras, or just because they feel like it. Often people in this camp spend their savings at an unsustainable rate. They're likely to exhaust their savings in their 70s or early 80s, when they might have many more years of life ahead of them.

I have friends and relatives in both camps, and I've encouraged them all to find the middle ground between these two camps: The first camp can spend more money and still feel safe about their money lasting, while the second camp should spend their money much more carefully to help make it last as long as they need it.

> *As you approach your retirement years,*
> *shift your thinking from saving money*
> *to building a diversified portfolio of*
> *risk-protected retirement income.*

If you're in one of these two camps now, you'll need to shift your thinking to reach this middle ground. To do so, you've got to start by changing your attitude toward your retirement savings. Throughout all your working years, you've (hopefully) been building a portfolio of retirement savings, without giving much thought to what you'll do with this money when you retire.

But now it's time to give that money the consideration it deserves, because you'll need to start drawing down your savings to support your life in retirement. To draw down your savings safely and responsibly, however, you need a plan that will sustain you throughout your potentially long life. The time has come for you to determine how to use your savings to build a portfolio of retirement income, one that reflects the realities of the 21st century. The *Spend Safely Strategy* can help you do that by providing a straightforward and simple way to build your portfolio of lifetime retirement income.

Understand the ABCs of the *Spend Safely in Retirement Strategy*

The *Spend Safely Strategy* is an overall approach to managing your income and spending during retirement. It can also help you make some of your most important retirement decisions.

Using the *Spend Safely Strategy*, you'll create a retirement income portfolio that includes your Social Security benefits, your pension (if you have one), and any savings you have in IRAs, 401(k) plans, or other retirement savings plans or accounts. Some of you may also have additional sources of retirement income, such as rental income. The money from all of these sources will be used to fund your retirement safely and responsibly.

The *Spend Safely Strategy* is based on recent research that I directed at the Stanford Center on Longevity, in collaboration with the Society of Actuaries. To determine effective methods for generating retirement income from savings, my fellow researchers and I systematically analyzed and compared 292 different retirement income strategies, using sophisticated analytical techniques that are commonly used to manage large pension plans. After months of analysis, we found that the *Spend Safely Strategy* was not only relatively straightforward for people to understand and implement, but also that the amount of retirement income it generated compared favorably to that of more complex strategies.

The baseline Spend Safely Strategy has three key steps:

 Step 1: Establish reliable monthly "retirement paychecks" that last the rest of your life, no matter how long you live, and don't drop if the stock market crashes. Building lifetime paychecks is critical because you could live a long time, given that nowadays many people are living into their mid to late 80s or 90s, and even to 100! These paychecks will be used either entirely or primarily to cover your basic living expenses, which are your "needs." These needs include housing costs, utility bills,

food, medical insurance premiums, and other essential expenses.

Most of you will use your Social Security benefits as the primary source of your retirement paychecks. (Some workers are employed by state and local governments that don't participate in Social Security, but they participate in their own pension plan.)

And since it's a critical part of your retirement portfolio, you'll learn how to maximize your lifetime Social Security income through a thoughtful delay strategy, which I explain later in this chapter. You may also have other possible sources of retirement paychecks, so I'll cover those, too, a little later in this book.

Step 2: Set up "retirement bonuses" to supplement your retirement paychecks. To implement this step, you'll use your retirement savings as a Retirement Income Generator (RIG) that will deliver a stream of lifetime retirement bonuses to supplement the money coming in from your Social Security benefits and any other retirement paychecks you may have. These bonuses have the potential to grow if times are good but might decrease periodically, or even go away completely, if times aren't good.

These bonuses can also be used to augment your retirement paychecks to cover your basic living expenses if you need additional funds. However, they're primarily to be used for paying for your discretionary purchases, or "wants." Wants are those living expenses you could reduce if necessary, such as the cost of traveling, hobbies, and spoiling your grandchildren.

Step 3: Build a cash stash. Set up a separate emergency fund at your bank or credit union. The money in this fund should be used to pay for predictable future expenses, such as home repairs, cars and car repairs, and updated appliances and furniture. It can also be used to pay for unforeseen emergencies, such as providing financial help to adult children and grandchildren, or to cover large, out-of-pocket medical or dental expenses. Separating this money from the rest of your retirement savings will help you avoid dipping into the part of your savings that generates your retirement paychecks and bonuses.

The appropriate amount of your cash stash could range from a few thousand dollars to a higher amount, depending on what makes you feel comfortable. This third step is the simplest—one that can be handled quickly and easily—so I won't go into any more detail in this book on setting up an emergency fund.

Note: If you've read my previous book, *Retirement Game-Changers,* you might recall that I described the *Spend Safely Strategy* in four steps in that book instead of three. As a result of the extensive research I conducted on the strategy after we published *Retirement Game-Changers*, I decided to condense the steps to just three in this book. It's still the same strategy, just refined. This book also provides many more details on the strategy, based on my recent research.

Before moving on to Chapters 2 through 4, where I'll explain the first two steps of the *Spend Safely Strategy* in more detail, I'd like to offer a brief explanation here of what these two steps involve. This will help you more quickly comprehend the concepts as you read the next three chapters.

Step 1: Maximize Social Security benefits to increase your paychecks

For most middle-income older workers and retirees, Social Security delivers the largest portion of their total retirement income—*at least one-half, and often two-thirds or more.* Social Security has unique advantages that protect against the common retirement planning risks facing most retirees:

- Social Security income protects against longevity risk by delivering a monthly income for the rest of your life, no matter how long you live.

- It also protects against inflation risk, since your benefits usually increase each year with the cost-of-living adjustment.

- Social Security protects against investment risk, too, since your benefits won't decrease if the stock market crashes.

- It also helps protect against the risk of cognitive decline or simply making mistakes in your later years, since you can deposit your monthly benefits automatically into your bank account each month. You don't need to make any decisions regarding investing this money or determining the amount of withdrawals you can make from your savings.

Social Security benefits also enjoy unique tax advantages. A portion of your Social Security income—often one-half or more—isn't subject to federal income taxes at all or to most state income taxes as well.

And finally, Social Security provides valuable survivor benefits that can protect the surviving spouse of a married couple.

Because of these advantages, it makes financial sense to maximize the risk-protected income you'll receive from this valuable benefit. Most people can maximize their Social Security by delaying the start of their benefits as long as they can, although there are no benefits to waiting beyond age 70.

With an effective delay strategy, it's possible to increase the Social Security income you receive throughout your life by $100,000 or more. So, it's a good use of your time to develop a strategy that will help you get the most from your Social Security benefits. Chapter 2 provides more details on Social Security and how to optimize the lifetime income you'll receive.

Step 2: Deploy your Retirement Income Generator (RIG) for your bonuses

For most retirees, Social Security income isn't enough money to finance a comfortable retirement, even if they've done what they can to optimize their Social Security benefits. For this reason, you'll want to supplement your Social Security income by using a portion of your savings to generate a stream of lifetime retirement bonuses to help cover your living expenses. For this step, you should think of your retirement savings as a lifetime RIG.

There are two things you'll need to do to set up your RIG:

1. Invest your retirement savings in a low-cost target date fund, balanced fund, or stock index fund, all of which are commonly available in many IRAs or 401(k) plans.

2. Set up a systematic withdrawal so you'll have money coming in on a regular basis from the fund or funds you've selected. The easiest way to calculate the annual amount that you can safely withdraw from savings for your retirement bonus is to use the IRS required minimum distribution (RMD) rates as a baseline. FYI: The RMD rules describe the *minimum* amount that you're required to withdraw from 401(k) plans and traditional IRAs.

    Due to recent changes in the law, the RMD rules apply to you at age 70½ if you were born on or before June 30, 1949, but at age 72 if you were born on or after July 1, 1949. (You'll find more on these rules in Chapter 3.) However, you have the freedom to withdraw higher amounts if that better meets your needs. You can also withdraw from your savings before the RMD rules apply to you. In either case, you want to make sure you don't withdraw so much that you might outlive your savings.

Our recent research shows that setting up your RIG, as described above, is a simple and reasonable way to generate retirement income that will last the rest of your life. Its effectiveness compares favorably to more complicated methods of generating retirement income.

Many IRA and 401(k) administrators can calculate the RMD for you and, once you retire, have that amount paid to you in the frequency you select (monthly, quarterly, or annually); this enables you to put your withdrawals on autopilot. And if you think you have to wait until the RMD rules apply to implement this strategy, you don't: If you retire before the RMD is required, you can still use the same IRS methodology to calculate your annual retirement bonus.

Chapters 3 and 4 contain details on how to use your IRA or the retirement savings plan you have through your job to generate a lifetime retirement income. These chapters also include information on the RMD withdrawal percentages you can choose to use before the RMD rules apply to you, considerations for investing your retirement savings, and examples that illustrate how to use the RMD to generate your retirement bonuses.

Subsequent chapters contain refinements and adjustments to the basic *Spend Safely Strategy* to reflect your goals and circumstances. For example, Chapter 5 shows how you can supplement Social Security benefits with additional risk-protected retirement paychecks.

Face up to common tough choices

When most people sit down to do the math and estimate the amount of the retirement paychecks and bonuses they'll be getting, they often realize they'll have less regular income coming in during retirement compared to when they were working. As a result, they have to decide whether they should work longer to increase their retirement income, lower their living expenses by spending less money, or do some combination of the two. The best decision for you will depend on your goals and circumstances.

Keep in mind that each person's situation will be unique. For instance, you might see a significant drop in your living expenses during retirement if your children have grown up and moved out, or if you've paid off your mortgage or downsized your residence. On the other hand, you might end up spending more in retirement if you decide to travel more, increase the amount or cost of your entertainment activities, or incur higher medical expenses.

To guide you to the decisions that make sense for you, you'll want to carefully think about your living expenses in retirement—both your needs and your wants. Some people might figure out how to reduce their living expenses as a price they're willing to pay for their retirement freedom. These people will focus on buying just enough to meet their needs and be happy. Others may decide to work longer so they can maintain the standard of living they currently enjoy. These people will need to decide if they want to ride out their working life at their current job or find another job that will make them happier and also provide the money they'll need to maintain their standard of living.

It's a highly personal choice. You'll need to spend some time doing your homework and consulting with your spouse or partner (if you have one) so you can make choices that offer a good balance between financial security and spending enough to make you happy. It's best that you make *informed* decisions and put in place solid plans that have a good chance of succeeding.

Plan together if you're married or partnered

If you're married or live with a partner, you'll want to set plans in place so that your retirement income lasts for the rest of *both* of your lives. Since this will influence all the decisions you read about in this book, it would be a good idea to read this book together. You'll also want to make sure you both understand the decisions you make, the reasons for them, the strategies you've adopted, and the location of the various sources of your retirement income. After all, the day might come when you or your spouse or partner passes away, and the other will need to continue to monitor the plans that you both put in place.

Speaking of your spouse or partner, make sure that all your beneficiary designations are up to date with any important retirement savings accounts you may have, including your 401(k) plan.

Decide if you want to work with an adviser

It's quite possible to implement the *Spend Safely Strategy* without requiring the involvement of a financial adviser. And that's good news for many people: Surveys show that most middle-income workers and retirees choose not to work with an adviser. This book will be most helpful to that group.

Of course, working with an adviser might make you feel more confident about your situation and the decisions you make, and they can help you develop a customized retirement plan. If you're interested in working with an adviser, take my advice and don't be sold by the first adviser you meet. Instead, go shopping for advisers who are trained in the complexities of generating retirement income and who are paid to have your best interests at heart. If possible, avoid working with advisers who earn high commissions or fees on the insurance or investment products they recommend to you. Look for advisers who will act as a fiduciary on your behalf; they will put your interests before their own interests. To get more details and ideas regarding working with a financial adviser, please see the guide titled *Get Help* on the "Bonus Chapters" page of www.restoflife.com.

One last thought: There are no perfect retirement income strategies. All strategies have their pros and cons, including the *Spend Safely Strategy*. It's entirely possible that an adviser or friend might recommend a different strategy that you'd like to consider. Before you make any decisions, compare the *Spend Safely Strategy* to any other strategies you're considering, and make an informed choice that's the best fit for you.

Replace worrying about retirement with solid plans

The *Spend Safely in Retirement Strategy* offers a strong, three-pronged approach to managing your retirement income and living expenses. It also keeps things simple for retirees by mirroring the money management strategies (paychecks, bonuses or overtime, cash stash) you most likely used while you were working.

Unfortunately, the economic crisis of 2020 created stress for many pre-retirees and retirees. However, developing a careful retirement income strategy is the best way to move beyond worrying and being anxious about your retirement finances. By carefully implementing the three steps described in this chapter, you'll feel much better about your future because you'll be off to a great start managing your money wisely!

Now that you have the big picture in mind, let's dig into the details, starting with Chapter 2, where you'll learn more about optimizing your Social Security benefits.

KEY TAKEAWAYS

▶ Carefully deploy your savings to generate a life-time retirement income that covers the cost of your living expenses.

▶ Start by maximizing the amount of risk-protected income you'll receive from Social Security over the course of your lifetime. This will most likely be the primary source of your retirement paychecks that will cover most, if not all, of your "needs"— your basic living expenses.

✗ ▶ Generate retirement bonuses to cover your "wants." To implement the baseline strategy, invest in a common, low-cost target date fund, balanced fund, or stock index fund, and use the IRS required minimum distribution (RMD) to determine the amount you can withdraw annually.

▶ Set up a cash stash, or emergency fund, to pay for both predictable and unpredictable future expenses that might cost more than your retirement paychecks and bonuses can easily cover.

savings acct.

Chapter 2

Take Your Social Security to the Max!

Deciding when to start your Social Security benefits is one of the most important financial decisions you'll make for the rest of your life. That's because it will have a significant impact on your financial security in your retirement years.

Many people just can't wait to start getting their Social Security income—they view it as free money that they're entitled to after paying Social Security taxes all their working lives. And while that last part is true, starting benefits as soon as possible is a big mistake for most people, often because they don't grasp the lifelong implications of their decision.

I often hear stories of older people who started their Social Security benefits as soon as they could, and as a result, they're receiving the minimum amount of Social Security income they could have received. Now that they're in their late 70s and 80s and are struggling financially, they regret their decision to start Social Security early.

Don't fall prey to the urban legends, myths, and folklore that you'll hear about Social Security—the stories that urge

17

you to start Social Security as early as possible or that Social Security won't be there for you when you need it. Instead, spend time determining the income you can expect to receive and learning how to get the most value from Social Security benefits over the course of your lifetime.

> *Starting Social Security benefits*
> *as soon as you can is a big mistake*
> *for most people.*

When it comes to financing your retirement, Social Security benefits have powerful, unique features:

- They're paid monthly for the rest of your life, no matter how long you live.
- They're increased for inflation each year.
- They won't drop in value if the stock market crashes.
- A portion of your benefits is exempt from income taxes.
- If you're married, Social Security pays valuable survivor benefits to your spouse.
- The system is user-friendly and helps protect against fraud and mistakes you might make if you mentally decline in your later years.

Simply put, Social Security is the best source for your retirement paychecks. Not a single other Retirement Income Generator has all the desirable features listed above.

For most middle-income workers, Social Security will deliver at least half, and often two-thirds or more, of their total retirement income. Since that's the case, it simply makes sense to maximize the value of those benefits, particularly if you're one of the millions of older workers who are approaching your retirement years with no meaningful benefits from a traditional pension plan.

With so much on the line, you'll want to spend the time it takes to learn how to get the most value out of Social Security, for both yourself and your spouse, if you're married. Don't let this necessary investment of time deter you—instead, commit to doing what you must to maximize this valuable benefit.

This chapter focuses on the simple steps you can take to maximize your Social Security benefits, which is Step 1 of the *Spend Safely Strategy*. It doesn't go into detail about Social Security's various rules and formulas, and it doesn't provide an in-depth look at every possible option—that's beyond the scope of this short book.

That's why I encourage you to learn more about Social Security, so you can better understand the strategies I've described in this chapter. My book, *Retirement Game-Changers*, devotes a lengthy chapter to summarizing Social Security benefits and the strategies you can use to get the most from them. You'll also learn a lot by visiting Social Security's helpful website, www.ssa.gov. And if you're really detail-oriented, you can read one of several other good books on Social Security that I've listed in the "Helpful Resources" section at the back of this book.

For our purposes here, your first step is to track down the estimate of your Social Security benefits that the Social Security Administration (SSA) mailed to you. It's a good starting point for learning more about Social Security.

Find your Social Security statement

Many of you may have received a statement in the mail from the SSA that includes estimates of your Social Security benefits. Rummage through your files to see if you can find the latest copy of that statement.

If you can't put your hands on it (or know you tossed it out), don't worry—you can view an online version of your statement by opening up a "my Social Security" account (at no charge) on the SSA website, www.ssa.gov. In fact, the SSA encourages citizens to go online—rather than wait for their paper statements—to learn about their estimated Social Security benefits.

Your Social Security Statement will show estimates of your monthly retirement income at three possible ages:

1. Age 62, the earliest possible age at which you can collect retirement benefits with the lowest monthly benefit
2. Your "full retirement age," which is between ages 66 and 67, depending on your birth year
3. Age 70, the latest age at which you can start retirement benefits with the maximum monthly benefit

Both the paper statements and your my Social Security account have a critical feature: They calculate the estimated Social Security income you can expect to get using your actual lifetime wage history. This gives you a much more accurate figure than some of the Social Security benefit calculators out there, which simply estimate your wage history.

Hopefully, seeing the estimates from the SSA will inspire you to get the most value from Social Security by learning even more about your options.

Find out how to maximize your lifetime Social Security income

Would you be interested in increasing your Social Security income by thousands of dollars per year? Over the course of your lifetime, your extra Social Security income could add up to more than $100,000! So, is it worth it to spend just a few hours learning how to secure this extra income? I'd say so!

You can potentially increase your lifetime payout from Social Security by $100,000 or more with a careful strategy to optimize your benefits.

Here's the easiest way to increase your Social Security income: For every month that you delay starting Social Security after age 62—but only up to age 70—you'll receive a permanent, lifetime increase in your monthly retirement income. By delaying the start of your monthly income, you can increase the total amount of money you can expect to receive from Social Security over the course of your lifetime.

If you're married, there are literally thousands of combinations for claiming Social Security benefits for yourself and your spouse. If you're single, there are more than a hundred possible strategies. No matter what your marital status is, because of the dozens of choices you face, you may have neither the time nor the expertise to decide what the best strategy for you would be. But it's the perfect application for a computer!

Fortunately, there are several online programs that can help you determine the optimum strategy for claiming your

Social Security benefits. A few of them are free, and some require a modest charge (these paid systems provide more details than the free systems). In either case, you should choose an online calculator that uses your actual wage history throughout your life to estimate your Social Security income. The "Helpful Resources" section at the end of this book identifies the online systems I'm familiar with that do this.

These systems usually ask a few simple questions about you and your spouse, if you're married. You'll also need to have handy the estimate of Social Security benefits that you received in the mail or from your online statement.

Usually these systems recommend that single workers or the primary wage-earner of a married couple delay the start of their benefits as long as possible, but not beyond age 70. For married couples, it's harder to make a generalized statement regarding the best strategy for the spouse who isn't the primary wage-earner. The optimal strategy for this spouse also varies considerably depending on the ages of both spouses and both of your work histories. With all these factors to consider, you can see why it's helpful to let a computer crank through all the possibilities and suggest the best strategy for you.

By comparing different options, these systems may show that you can increase your expected lifetime payout from Social Security by $100,000 or more. For married couples, delaying Social Security benefits for the primary wage-earner has an important added advantage: It often increases the survivor's benefit for the other spouse after the primary wage-earner passes away. With so much money at stake, it's well worth your time to use and understand the results of one of these systems. It can also be a good use of your money to pay for one of the more detailed systems.

If you're working with a financial adviser, ask if they're trained on claiming Social Security benefits. Some advisers have taken training to help their clients with this important task.

WARNING

If a potential adviser urges you to claim Social Security benefits as soon as possible and invest your Social Security benefits with them, alarm bells should be ringing! In most cases, that's not even remotely close to the best strategy to help you get the most out of Social Security. Such an adviser is either uninformed about Social Security or may care more about maximizing their income by encouraging you to either invest your Social Security benefits with them or buy an insurance product that pays them a fat commission. If you're getting this advice, find another adviser.

Manage the gap between when you retire and the start of Social Security benefits

Suppose you determine that the best time to start your Social Security benefits is after the age at which you want to retire. Now what?

If you retire before the optimal age at which to start your Social Security benefits, you can use one of two options that will enable you to delay your Social Security benefits until your optimal age:

1. Estimate the monthly income you'd receive from Social Security should you start benefits immediately after you

retire. Then find a way to earn just enough money from working or self-employment to enable you to delay your Social Security benefits until your optimal age.

2. Use a portion of your retirement savings to fund a "Social Security bridge payment," which will substitute for your estimated Social Security income until you reach your optimal age. A lot of research, including research that I've conducted, demonstrates that such a bridge strategy is one of the best ways to use your retirement savings.

To fund your Social Security bridge payment, you can use investments that are commonly offered in IRAs and 401(k) plans and protect against investment volatility. Examples include short-term bond funds, money market funds, CDs, and stable value funds.

Note: If you've read my previous book, *Retirement Game-Changers,* you might recall that I described a "retirement transition fund"; that fund included a Social Security bridge payment but also addressed other goals.

One last thought: Delaying the start of your Social Security benefits until age 70 is often the strategy recommended by both experts and the online systems discussed earlier in this chapter. However, this isn't an all-or-nothing decision. You'll still realize an improvement in your retirement finances with any delay in starting your benefits past age 62, even if it's just for a few years.

As an ongoing, secure source of income, Social Security will be the foundation of your retirement paychecks. However, if you want more risk-protected retirement income than what will be provided by Social Security—even after you've taken it to the max—see Chapter 5 for some ideas and strategies that will help you achieve that goal.

▼

How Bob will optimize his Social Security benefits

Bob decides to retire at age 65. As part of his planning, he does his homework to determine the optimal age to start his Social Security benefits. He calculates that if he were to start his Social Security income at age 65, he would receive $2,000 per month, or $24,000 per year. But if he waits to start his Social Security benefits until age 70, he estimates his Social Security income would be $2,862 per month, or $34,344 per year. He decides that waiting until age 70 is the best strategy for him.

Bob has two effective options to replace the $2,000-a-month Social Security payment he would have received starting at age 65 until he reaches age 70 and begins receiving Social Security benefits. His first option is to continue working just enough after age 65 to replace the Social Security benefits he's delaying. In this case, he would need to earn an amount that allows him to clear $2,000 per month, after considering income taxes.

Alternatively, if Bob doesn't want to continue working after he reaches age 65, his second option would be to set up a Social Security bridge fund that would provide him with a monthly payment to substitute for the $2,000 monthly Social Security benefit he's delaying. Since Bob would be deferring his Social

Security benefit for five years, he would need to set aside $120,000 from his retirement savings ($24,000 x five years) in his Social Security bridge fund. He could then withdraw $2,000 per month from this account until age 70, when his Social Security benefits kick in.

In order to implement this strategy, it would be best for Bob to set aside and invest the $120,000 separately from the retirement savings he uses to generate his retirement bonuses. This protects his Social Security bridge payment against stock market volatility, similar to Social Security's protections. To do this, he could invest the money in a short-term bond fund or a stable value fund. He could also use interest earnings from this account to increase his Social Security bridge payment in future years.

One quick note: If the money in Bob's Social Security bridge fund is from pre-tax savings, he might want to increase his Social Security bridge payment so that, after paying income taxes, he still nets $2,000.

Another note: In the scenario above, Bob sets up his Social Security bridge fund to pay him his expected age 65 Social Security payment of $2,000 per month between ages 65 and 70. When his actual Social Security benefit starts, he's going to enjoy a raise to his expected age 70 Social Security benefit of $2,862 per month. If he would like his Social Security bridge fund to pay him his expected age 70 benefit between ages 65 and 70, he'll need to create a larger Social Security bridge fund to account for the larger monthly amount he'll be withdrawing.

Don't fall for the myth that Social Security won't be there when you need it

A common concern I hear about Social Security is that it will go bankrupt in the 2030s because the Social Security Trust Fund is projected to be exhausted at that time. The fear is that if this happens, you might not receive *anything* from Social Security. Some people use this fear as justification for starting their Social Security benefits as soon as possible.

To set the record straight, it's just not possible for Social Security to go completely bankrupt as long as current workers are paying their FICA taxes into the system. In the worst-case scenario, if the Trust Fund *is* exhausted and Congress doesn't act to shore up Social Security, in theory, you could receive a reduction of 20% to 25% in your Social Security benefits. While that would certainly be bad news, it's highly unlikely that a time will come when you'll receive *nothing* from Social Security.

In addition, even if your Social Security benefits are reduced in the future, optimizing your benefits through a delay strategy will most likely still be the best way to maximize the Social Security income you'll receive over the course of your lifetime. Because even in the unlikely event that Congress allows a future reduction in Social Security benefits, you won't escape the reduction just because you started your benefits early.

If you're interested in learning more about the viability of Social Security, see the online columns and papers I've identified in the "Helpful Resources" section at the back of this book.

Learning how to take Social Security to the max is a very important step on your path to financial resilience in retirement. Be Social Security smart: Learn all you can to make careful, informed decisions.

Next up? Using your retirement savings to set up your Retirement Income Generators.

KEY TAKEAWAYS

▶ Social Security protects against inflation and investment losses, and it's paid for the rest of your life, no matter how long you live.

▶ It's smart to maximize your lifetime Social Security benefits because they're the best source of risk-protected retirement income for most workers.

▶ You can maximize your lifetime Social Security benefits with a thoughtful strategy to delay starting your benefits.

▶ There are two ways to delay starting Social Security: Work just enough so that you don't need Social Security to cover your living expenses until you begin receiving your benefits, or set up a Social Security bridge payment fund with a portion of your existing retirement savings.

Chapter 3

Use Your Savings to Generate Lifetime Retirement Income

Determining how to invest and withdraw money from your savings during retirement so that you don't run out of funds is one of the most complex and high-stakes retirement decisions you'll face. Withdraw too fast or experience poor investment returns, and you could outlive your savings. Withdraw too cautiously or experience favorable investment returns, and you could leave the earth with a lot of money in the bank, money you could have spent while you were still alive.

I make these points not to scare you but to encourage you to learn more about your options. Many attendees at my retirement planning workshops feel much better when they learn about reasonable strategies to effectively deploy their retirement savings. Information is power!

In fact, we developed the *Spend Safely Strategy* to provide readers like you with a straightforward way to more easily make these decisions. You don't need to have a degree in financial management to understand this strategy—you can easily implement it using investment options that are commonly found in IRA platforms and employer-sponsored savings plans, such as 401(k) plans.

This chapter describes Step 2 of the *Spend Safely Strategy* and offers information on the methods you can use to deploy your Retirement Income Generator (RIG) and determine the amount of your annual retirement bonuses. The next chapter, which also covers Step 2 of the strategy, goes into more detail regarding the investing strategies you can use to generate your retirement bonuses. These bonuses will supplement your guaranteed retirement paychecks from Social Security, which make up Step 1 of the *Spend Safely Strategy*.

Before we dig into the recommended *Spend Safely Strategy* method of determining the amount of your retirement bonuses, let's take a high-level look at systematic withdrawals and how they work.

Learn the basics of systematic withdrawals

As I mentioned in Chapter 1, you'll use your retirement savings to establish a RIG that will deliver a stream of lifetime retirement bonuses through a series of systematic withdrawals. "Systematic withdrawals" is the technical term for the process of investing your savings and using a disciplined method to take money out of your retirement savings accounts to pay for your expenses. When you set up your own systematic withdrawals, the main goal is to invest your savings and then withdraw the investment earnings and principal cautiously, so that you don't outlive your assets. You can set up systematic withdrawals using most IRAs and many 401(k) plans.

When using a systematic withdrawal method, you must decide how much to withdraw and how often to withdraw it—monthly, quarterly, or annually—from the amount of savings you've invested for this purpose. Then you'll need to notify your IRA or 401(k) administrator about your withdrawal strategy so they'll automatically pay you the amounts on schedule. You'll also need to monitor your investment strategy and potentially readjust your withdrawal amounts in order to make your savings last for the rest of your life.

One simple way to implement systematic withdrawals is to choose a basic annual withdrawal percentage, such as 3%, 4%, 5%, or even 6%, and set up your accounts to pay you that amount on whatever schedule you prefer. Be aware that choosing your own withdrawal percentage is a "pay me now or pay me later" decision. A higher withdrawal percentage will provide more income in the early years of your retirement than a lower withdrawal percentage would, but a higher percentage also increases the risk that your retirement income could be reduced substantially in later years. Using a higher withdrawal percentage also reduces the value of any remaining assets that can be a legacy once you've passed away, if that's important to you.

It's important to note that there's not a single magic withdrawal percentage that will work for everybody. Keeping that in mind, you'll want to carefully consider and choose the withdrawal strategy that best suits your preferences for the "pay me now or pay me later" goal and for a potential legacy.

Something important you'll need to keep in mind: One critical risk when using systematic withdrawals is the so-called "sequence of returns" risk. This happens when you continue making significant withdrawals from your principal after the stock market drops, and you end up withdrawing too much from your remaining principal. If you do this, you may not have enough savings remaining to fully recover when the stock market bounces back.

> *It's best to readjust your annual withdrawal amount each year to reflect investment gains or losses that have occurred.*

To address this risk, it's best to readjust your annual withdrawal amount each year to reflect the investment gains or losses that have occurred in the past 12 months. To do so, you'll recalculate the amount of your withdrawal each year by applying your withdrawal percentage to the value of your remaining savings at the beginning of each year. I know this might sound complicated, but keep reading; you'll see how to set up these adjustments to be made automatically.

With these adjustments to your withdrawal amounts, if your assets enjoy good investment returns, you can increase your withdrawals. On the other hand, you'll want to reduce your withdrawals if your assets lose money. That's a key reason to use retirement bonuses less for critical living expenses and more for discretionary expenses, which you can cut back on if necessary.

Now that you know a bit more about systematic withdrawals, I hope you're not feeling overwhelmed knowing that you'll have to monitor your investments and adjust your withdrawal amounts to ensure that you don't run through your savings too quickly. If you're feeling that you may be in over your head, understand that you're not: The *Spend Safely Strategy's* recommended systematic withdrawal method for generating retirement bonuses is fairly simple to implement and maintain.

Let's discuss the details of it now.

Understand the required minimum distribution method and rules

For most tax-advantaged retirement accounts—401(k)s, 403(b)s, 457(b)s, and deductible IRAs (but not Roth IRAs)— Uncle Sam wants to make sure that you eventually pay income taxes on the pre-tax money you saved in these accounts. So our good uncle employs the required minimum distribution (RMD) rules that specify the minimum amounts you must withdraw from your retirement savings each year and include in your taxable income.

Due to changes in the law adopted in December 2019, the RMD rules first apply to you for the calendar year during which you turn age 70½, provided you reached that age before December 31, 2019. This means you were born on or before June 30, 1949. If you were born on or after July 1, 1949, the RMD rules will apply to you starting with the calendar year you turn age 72.

The RMD can be a reasonable, straightforward method for generating retirement bonuses that last the rest of your life. This conclusion has been confirmed not only by recent research reports I've published (identified in the "Helpful Resources" section) but also by other respected researchers.

One advantage of using the RMD to determine your withdrawal strategy is that the amount of your retirement bonus will be automatically adjusted up or down from year to year, depending on your investment returns. Since the *Spend Safely Strategy* covers most, if not all, of your basic living expenses with your secure retirement paychecks, the RMD withdrawal strategy helps ensure that you won't have to move in with your kids if your retirement bonus drops because of poor investment returns.

There's another significant advantage to using the RMD rules to determine your retirement bonuses: Virtually any IRA or 401(k) administrator can calculate the amount of the RMD for you, and many can even pay it automatically to you in the frequency you specify (monthly, quarterly, or annually). This way, you can put your retirement bonuses on autopilot. And, at the beginning of each year, your IRA or 401(k) plan administrator can tell you the amount of your bonus for the coming year, which will help you plan your spending for the year.

While you'd have to be a tax accountant to understand all the intricacies of the RMD rules, the basic concepts are fairly straightforward to understand if you take the time to study them. If you're interested in more details on the RMD, please see the bonus chapter titled *Navigate the Tax Rules* on the "Bonus Chapters" page of www.restoflife.com.

Here's the bottom line: Using the RMD can simplify the process of generating retirement bonuses for retirees who don't want to use more complex strategies or work with a financial adviser. That's why it's an important part of the *Spend Safely Strategy*.

ℹ️ FOR MORE DETAILS

· ·

Learn about RMD withdrawal percentages

The RMD rules result in a series of withdrawal percentages, or payout rates, that start when the rules apply to you. FYI: In late 2019, the IRS proposed new regulations that would slightly decrease the RMD withdrawal percentages; these lower percentages would begin to apply in 2021 and thereafter. The RMD withdrawal percentages currently in effect will continue to apply during 2020.

As of the date of this book's publication, finalizing these rules has been delayed due to the pandemic of 2020. Check the "Bonus Chapters" page of www.restoflife.com for updates on the status of these regulations.

Under the rules that would begin to apply in 2021, the RMD withdrawal percentages would start at 3.6630% for people age 72 and then would increase each year thereafter (see the following table for the exact amounts). For any given calendar year, you'll apply the annual payout rate to the value of your assets as of the previous December 31. As a result, you'll know exactly how much you're required to withdraw in the coming year. The table on the following page also shows the payout rates you can use before the RMD rules apply to you if you use the same methodology as the IRS RMD.

Note: You can always safely use the current RMD withdrawal percentages, even if the proposed rules are finalized. In this case, the current RMD withdrawal percentages would produce withdrawal amounts that would be slightly higher than the minimum amounts that would be required under the new rules.

FYI: The Coronavirus Aid, Relief, and Economic Security Act that was passed in March 2020 suspended the RMD requirements for 2020 only. As of the publication date of this book, the RMD rules will again apply in 2021.

TABLE 3.1. Withdrawal percentages using the IRS required minimum distribution methodology

Age	Payout Rates for 2020	Proposed Payout Rates for 2021 and After	Age	Payout Rates for 2020	Proposed Payout Rates for 2021 and After
60	2.7174%*	2.5907%*	76	4.5455%	4.2194%
61	2.7933%*	2.6525%*	77	4.7170%	4.3860%
62	2.8653%*	2.7248%*	78	4.9261%	4.5662%
63	2.9499%*	2.7933%*	79	5.1282%	4.7619%
64	3.0303%*	2.8736%*	80	5.3476%	4.9505%
65	3.1250%*	2.9586% *	81	5.5866%	5.1813%
66	3.2152%*	3.0395%*	82	5.8480%	5.4348%
67	3.3113%*	3.1250%*	83	6.1350%	5.6818%
68	3.4247%*	3.2258%*	84	6.4516%	5.9524%
69	3.5336%*	3.3223%*	85	6.7568%	6.2500%
70	3.6496%	3.4364%*	86	7.0922%	6.5789%
71	3.7736%	3.5461%*	87	7.4627%	6.9444%
72	3.9063%	3.6630%	88	7.8740%	7.3529%
73	4.0486%	3.7879%	89	8.3333%	7.7519%
74	4.2017%	3.9216%	90	8.7719%	8.2645%
75	4.3669%	4.0650%			

NOTES:

- The payout rates marked with an * above for ages 60 through 69 for the 2020 rates and ages 60 through 71 for the 2021 rates aren't required by the IRS rules. However, they've been calculated using the same methodology as the RMD.

- This table is for illustration purposes; the RMD table continues beyond age 90.

- To determine the payout rate you should be applying for a given calendar year, use the age you turn on your birthday during the applicable calendar year.

- The RMD payout percentages apply to the named account holder on each IRA or 401(k) account. If you're part of a married couple, the applicable withdrawal percentage for each account will still depend on the age of the named account holder with one key exception: If you're married and your spouse is more than 10 years younger than you, a table with different payout rates applies.

- You must withdraw the RMD amount that applies for a calendar year by December 31 of that year. However, there is a grace period until the April 1 following the first year that the RMD rules apply. Thereafter, the required minimum withdrawal amount for a year must be made by December 31 to avoid penalties.

Table 3.1 illustrates one feature of the RMD methodology that's important to understand. This payout method "backloads" your retirement income into your later years, by starting with low payout rates in your 60s and 70s that then increase each year throughout retirement. If you want to refine the *Spend Safely Strategy* to accelerate your retirement income in the earlier years of your retirement, see Chapters 5, 6, and 8 for effective strategies you can implement.

$1079.56/mo. Vavinport
363.64 mo Voya
$1443.20/mo

12954.68 DAV
4454.59 Voya
17409.27 yr

_____

▼

How the RMD methodology will work for Ellen

Here are a few RMD examples for a hypothetical woman named Ellen to help you more clearly understand the RMD rules and how they work. Try to work through each of the examples—they'll help you understand the basic concepts. For the purpose of these examples, we'll use the proposed rules that would apply in 2021 and after.

Ellen turns 72 on September 1, 2021. This means she'll reach age 72 during 2021, and the RMD rules will apply to her for the first time that year. As of December 31, 2020, the value of her total retirement savings will be $400,000. The RMD rules for a 72-year-old require that Ellen withdraw 3.6630% of her savings during 2021. Multiplying $400,000 by .036630 results in a withdrawal amount, aka retirement bonus, of $14,652 for 2021.

Now suppose that the value of Ellen's retirement savings at the end of 2021 is $420,000, after taking into account the saving withdrawals she made that year as well as the investment earnings she made on her savings. In this case, the RMD rules for a 73-year-old require Ellen to withdraw 3.7879% of $420,000 during 2022. Multiplying $420,000 by .037879 would result in a retirement bonus of $15,909 for 2022.

Finally, let's suppose Ellen's investments lose money during 2022, and by the end of that year, her savings are valued at $380,000, which reflects the withdrawals she made during 2022 as well as her investment losses. In this case, the RMD rules for a 74-year-old require Ellen to withdraw 3.9216% of $380,000 during 2023. Multiplying $380,000 by .039216 would result in a retirement bonus for Ellen of $14,902 for 2023.

Explore possible work-arounds

It's entirely reasonable that many people will want or need to start drawing from their retirement savings before age 72. For example, some people who are delaying their Social Security benefits until age 70 might decide that age 70 is also a good time to begin withdrawing money from their savings. For these people, using the RMD percentages to determine their withdrawal percentage before the RMD rules actually apply to them is a good option.

There are two situations you may face if you decide to retire before the RMD rules apply to you and want to use the RMD methodology to calculate the amount of your retirement bonuses.

In the first situation, you may have to determine the amount of your retirement bonus on your own. That's because while many IRA and 401(k) administrators can calculate and pay the RMD for you, some may not be set up to implement the RMD methodology before it's required for you. In that case, you'll need to calculate the amount of your own retirement bonus, then tell your IRA or 401(k) administrator the amount you want paid to you for the year as well as the frequency of the payment (monthly, quarterly, or in one annual payment).

In the second situation, let's also suppose you want to retire before the RMD rules apply to you and before the optimal age to start your Social Security benefits. In this case, you would want to pay yourself both a Social Security bridge payment (as described in Chapter 2) and an RMD retirement bonus. It's possible that some IRA and 401(k) administrators may not be able to handle two separate payments from your savings. In this case, you'll need to calculate the total amount of both payments and tell your IRA or 401(k) administrator the total amount you want to have paid to you from your savings for the year.

If you feel uncomfortable making the above calculations on your own, you might want to work with your tax accountant or a financial adviser to help you figure it out.

Consider these ideas if implementing systematic withdrawals seems too complicated

After reading this chapter and the next chapter on investing, you might decide that implementing systematic withdrawals on your own is just too complicated for you.

In this case, in order to generate consistent retirement paychecks, one possibility would be to use part of your savings to buy an annuity, a refinement of the *Spend Safely Strategy* that's described in more detail in Chapter 5. The insurance company from which you purchase the annuity will invest the money you used to purchase the annuity and automatically pay you a lifetime retirement paycheck that doesn't decrease when the stock market declines. This option is also straightforward because annuities automatically comply with the IRS RMD rules.

Another user-friendly option for implementing systematic withdrawals is to use a managed payout fund that does the investing for you, calculates the amount of the annual bonus, and automatically pays you that amount. Examples of this type of fund include Fidelity's Income Replacement Funds, Schwab's Monthly Income Funds, and Vanguard's Managed Payout Fund.

You could also work with an advisory service, such as Betterment, Edelman Financial Engines, or United Income, that will implement systematic withdrawals for you. Financial institutions such as Fidelity Investments, Schwab, and Vanguard also offer these services. And you might even find such a service already exists in your 401(k) plan.

If you're interested in any of these alternatives, take the time to shop around. Each fund or service has its own investment strategies, methods for calculating the annual withdrawal amount, and fees for performing this service for you. Be sure you do your research before handing over your money to make sure you're making the best choice for you.

Also note that with a managed payout fund or advisory service, you'll still need to comply with the RMD rules described in this chapter, if your savings are subject to these rules. In this case, you'll also want to determine if the fund administrator or advisory service can help you comply with these rules.

1 - RMD - bonus payout
2. annuity
3 - managed payout fund
4 - advisory service

⚠ WARNING

In December 2019, Congress passed the SECURE Act, which requires 401(k) plans to provide their plan participants with an estimate of the retirement income their accounts might generate. If you receive such a statement from your 401(k) provider, look it over carefully: These statements can be helpful because they give you a ballpark estimate of the retirement income you might receive from your 401(k) plan.

However, they can also create a trap for the unwary. Here's the problem: The amount of your *estimated* retirement income can vary substantially from the *actual* amount of retirement income you'll receive when you deploy your savings to start generating retirement income.

There are several reasons for this discrepancy. For example, when preparing these retirement income estimates, 401(k) providers often assume you'll buy an annuity with your entire account balance. But not all retirees will make that choice, because they decide to allocate their savings among a few different Retirement Income Generators (RIGs) to meet various goals they have for their retirement income.

There are two more challenges that occur with these estimated retirement income statements. The first involves the fact that in order to create these estimates, 401(k) providers need to make an assumption about the age at which you'll retire. But this age could be different from your actual retirement age. In addition, they need to make an assumption regarding the rate of return that your account will earn between the date of the statement and your assumed retirement date. Again, the rate of return your account will actually earn could be very different from the assumed rate of return. The differences between these two assumptions and your actual experience mean the retirement income statements could miss the mark, sometimes significantly.

Here's the bottom line: Don't blindly count on receiving the amount of income you might see in your 401(k) retirement income estimate. Instead, as you approach retirement, take the time to do your homework, including understanding the various assumptions that were made to prepare your statement of estimated retirement income. Also, determine how your actual retirement income might differ from this estimate based on the RIGs you select to best meet your goals and circumstances. By taking time to do the math, you'll have a much more accurate picture of the retirement income you can expect to receive.

Whew! I know there's a lot to digest in this chapter, but it's well worth your time to understand the basic concepts. Remember: You're planning your financial security for the rest of your life. You may even need to reread this chapter to let it all sink in.

The next chapter discusses investment strategies for implementing your retirement bonuses using the RMD methodology. Hang in there—you're doing great!

KEY TAKEAWAYS

▶ If you're using systematic withdrawals to determine your retirement bonus, it's best to review your investment returns annually and then increase or decrease your withdrawals from savings to reflect your investment experience each year.

▶ Using the IRS required minimum distribution (RMD) to calculate the amount you withdraw from savings each year is a simple, effective way to make your savings last for the rest of your life.

▶ If you'd rather not deal with the complexities of investing and drawing down your retirement savings, consider annuities, managed payout funds, or services that will do it for you.

Chapter 4

Invest Carefully for Growth

Now that you know how the RMD methodology works, it's time to learn about the investment strategies you can put in place to generate your retirement bonuses.

Investing your savings to generate these bonuses involves two key goals: You'll want to determine an investment strategy that provides a potential for growth in the amount of your retirement bonus, yet is also not too risky and allows you to sleep soundly at night. This chapter helps you balance these two goals.

In Chapters 1 and 2, we discussed the key elements of the Social Security retirement paycheck that becomes the "guaranteed" part of your retirement income portfolio. This money is protected against longevity risk, inflation risk, and investment risk. And if you optimize your Social Security benefits, as described in Chapter 2, then it's highly likely that a very high percentage—well over half, and possibly two-thirds or more—of your total retirement income will be protected against the most common retirement investing risks.

This risk-protection should help give you the confidence to view your retirement bonuses as the part of your retirement income portfolio with which you can take some calculated investing risks in exchange for the potential for growth. Your important task now is to determine the portion of your retirement savings you'll invest in the stock market. By making this decision carefully, you should be able to move past the worry and anxiety of managing your retirement funds, and feel comfortable and confident enough to go enjoy your retirement life.

Understand this key dilemma regarding investing in stocks

Investing in stocks presents a significant dilemma for retirement investors. History has demonstrated that stocks can deliver higher returns than other investments *most of the time but not always*. It's this "but not always" aspect of investing that presents the dilemma.

(For the purposes of this discussion, investing in a mutual fund or pooled fund in your 401(k) plan that primarily invests in stocks counts as "investing in stocks.")

On the one hand, many respected research studies support investing a significant portion of your retirement savings in stocks for growth potential, after you've established a floor of guaranteed retirement income. On the other hand, this assumes you can tolerate the resulting volatility in this part of your retirement income portfolio.

That's why I recommend choosing a strategy that maximizes your Social Security income, which you'll use to cover your essential living expenses. Then you'll use your retirement bonuses primarily to pay for discretionary living expenses. With this strategy in place, if you experience poor investment returns, you can hopefully reduce your spending on the discretionary expenses without having to worry about paying for the essential expenses.

If you decide to adopt this strategy, you could invest your retirement savings in one of the following funds:

- A stock index fund (such funds are usually invested almost 100% in stocks)
- A balanced fund (such funds are often invested one-third to two-thirds in stocks)
- A target date fund (such funds are often invested about 50% in stocks by the time you reach retirement age)

These funds are commonly offered in IRA platforms and 401(k) plans, making it easy for retirees to invest in them. The asset allocation with different balanced funds and target date funds can vary significantly, so it's a good idea to carefully read and understand the descriptions and disclosures that these funds typically provide.

As described in Chapter 3, the RMD methodology calls for increasing your withdrawals when investment returns are good but decreasing your withdrawals when investment returns are poor. The higher the percentage of your retirement savings that's devoted to stocks, the greater your *expected* future returns will be and the greater your future retirement bonus *might* be. Of course, the phenomenon works both ways: If the stock market declines, then the higher percentage of your savings you invested in the stock market usually results in higher losses—and higher necessary reductions in your spending.

Learn about the potential for growth in retirement bonuses through stock investing

Research that I've conducted illustrates that over time, investing significantly in stocks can increase your retirement bonuses by substantial amounts. During our research, we looked at returns for various historical periods, and over some of these periods, we found that the retirement bonus amounts doubled or even tripled over time.

This same research also revealed a few historical periods when stocks didn't substantially outperform bonds, and even periods when the retirement bonus amount decreased by 30% or more. In some of these cases, however, the retirement bonus amount after the decrease was still higher than what the bonus amount would have been if the retiree had invested in bonds throughout retirement. The reason is that the decrease followed a period of much higher increases in the bonus amount, due to favorable investment performance leading up to the period when the stock market then decreased.

The stock market downturn in 2020 resulting from the COVID-19 pandemic is the latest example of this phenomenon. The stock market dropped in the first half of 2020, following a bull market that had lasted more than 10 years. Most workers and retirees who had invested significantly in the stock market during the 10-year bull market were still ahead when compared to investing in bonds, even reflecting the stock market losses in 2020.

If you want to review research that illustrates these points and supports the investment suggestions in this chapter, please see the bonus chapter titled *Stock Investing in Retirement—Opportunity and Risk* on the "Bonus Chapters" page of www.restoflife.com. It will provide you with a good idea of how much your income might fluctuate up and down with stock investments.

Seek low-cost investments

Do you think you need to be an investing genius or spend lots of time deciding how to invest your retirement savings in order to generate positive returns? That really isn't necessary. Instead, let me introduce you to a game-changing way of thinking that can simplify your retirement investments. I'll offer my own opinions—based on years of study and research—although I acknowledge that other experts may have different opinions based on their own education and research.

Reputable studies demonstrate that over the long run, you'll most likely earn a higher rate of return on your investment by investing in low-cost index funds. Low-cost index funds simply invest in all the stocks or bonds in a particular index without trying to pick winners or sell losers.

For the purposes of our discussion here, I'm defining a low-cost mutual fund or index fund as having an "expense ratio" of less than 0.20% per year, although the lower it is, the better (you can find funds with expense ratios of 0.10% or lower). Many 401(k) plans and some IRA providers offer a choice of low-cost index funds. These funds may invest exclusively in stocks or may offer a mix of stocks and bonds. Your 401(k) plan or IRA providers might also offer index funds that invest in bonds, international stocks, or real estate investment trusts (REITs) that invest in commercial real estate. These types of funds could also be good choices for the benefit of our discussion here.

> Studies demonstrate that over the long run, you'll most likely earn a higher rate of return by investing in low-cost index funds. This makes investing your retirement savings a lot simpler. The added bonus? Investing in low-cost funds has the potential to increase your savings by thousands of dollars over your lifetime, which will increase your retirement bonuses in the process!

As a result of their straightforward investing strategy, investment costs for these types of funds are generally very low. Interestingly enough, such funds have usually outperformed mutual funds that have a fund manager who actively manages the investments, or the results you'd get after paying an adviser to select investments they think will do well.

It might seem counterintuitive that index funds would outperform funds where professionals actively try to buy winners and sell losers. Studies have shown, however, that paying someone to select and monitor investments doesn't usually result in higher returns credited to your savings after taking into account the fees or commissions paid to the professionals to actively manage the investments.

Using low-cost index funds actually makes investing a lot simpler—you don't have to deal with complex strategies, and you aren't required to work with investment advisers. You also don't need to spend a lot of time in a futile effort to find the absolute best investments. Instead, you can feel comfortable simply investing in the low-cost index funds that are commonly offered in many IRAs and 401(k) plans, or through investment institutions such as Fidelity Investments, Schwab, and Vanguard.

Workers who have a 401(k) plan through a large employer (one with 1,000 or more employees) will find that low-cost index mutual funds are commonly included in the 401(k) investment options. That's because the plan administrators typically hire experts to shop for low-cost funds that are appropriate for retirement investing. If you've worked for a large employer and your 401(k) plan has these types of funds, there's no reason you should roll your money out of your employer's 401(k) plan when you retire. In fact, your employer's 401(k) plan can also protect you against fraudsters who want to steal your retirement savings, a protection you might not enjoy with other investments.

The 401(k) plans of smaller employers, typically those with less than 100 employees, may not have the resources to shop for the best funds or might offer funds with high expenses (1% or higher). In this case, when you retire, you're most likely better off rolling your savings into a low-cost IRA available from such companies as Fidelity Investments, Schwab, or Vanguard.

Before choosing to move your money, however, be sure to review your 401(k) plan disclosures to determine the expenses of the funds it offers. You may find that the funds you're invested in are reputable and have annual expenses of 0.20% or lower. If that's the case, you may not need to roll your money over to a different financial institution.

🄋 **WARNING**

All mutual funds, IRAs, and 401(k) plans are required to disclose the expense ratios of their funds. If you can't easily find these disclosures in your paperwork or online, ask the provider or investment adviser for them. If they don't give them to you, that's a red flag that you should invest elsewhere.

One caveat: The low-cost investments discussed in this chapter should work well for middle-income retirees with less than $1 million in retirement savings who have built a sufficient portfolio of retirement paychecks. If you have more than $1 million in savings, it could be worthwhile for you to work with an adviser who could help you determine an appropriate mix between stocks and bonds, and then help you select and monitor your retirement investments. Just make sure any adviser you work with not only has the training and expertise to help you generate retirement income from your savings, but also is not influenced by any commissions or fees they might receive by selling you certain investments or insurance products.

Be ready to ride out the inevitable ups and downs of the stock market

No matter what type of investments you make in the stock market, there's one key guideline you need to follow: In the event of a stock market crash, don't panic and immediately sell all your stocks or mutual funds.

It can be hard for retirees to maintain this discipline since you might not be able to make up your losses, even if you go back to work. However, history has shown it's not a wise move to make. By selling all your investments after a stock market crash, you lock in your losses and don't give your assets a chance to recover, which history has shown has happened repeatedly with prior stock market crashes.

Covering your basic living expenses with risk-protected income should give you the confidence to ride out the inevitable stock market downturns that will occur during the rest of your life.

It's generally best just to ride out the stock market declines so that you're invested when the stock market recovers. To help you follow this guideline, be sure to cover your basic living expenses with guaranteed retirement paychecks, such as Social Security benefits, that continue to be paid no matter what happens in the stock market. If you need even more risk-protected income after you've optimized Social Security, consider using a portion of your savings to buy an annuity, as discussed more in the next chapter.

Building a floor of risk-protected income with Social Security and an annuity should give you the confidence to ride out the inevitable stock market downturns that will occur during the rest of your life. When the stock market crashes again at some point in the future—and chances are good that it will—this strategy will hopefully provide tremendous relief and allow you to sleep well at night.

Here's one more strategy that can help you ride out stock market downturns: Estimate the amount of the retirement bonuses that you anticipate withdrawing from your savings in the next one to three years. Place this amount in investments that don't drop when the stock market declines, such as money market funds, short-term bond funds, and stable value funds. This way, you protect the withdrawals you'll make soon, and you'll also enable the rest of your savings to remain invested for the long term.

Congratulate yourself on learning the basics

Now that you've learned the basic ideas for building your retirement income portfolio of paychecks and bonuses, it's time to move on to Section 2, which discusses straightforward refinements and adjustments you can make to personalize your strategy for the specific goals and circumstances you might have.

For instance, if at any time you no longer want to manage your investments or if you desire more risk-protected retirement income, you can always simplify your retirement income portfolio by using part of your savings to buy a simple, cost-effective single premium immediate annuity (SPIA). Chapter 5 discusses that possibility in detail.

Building your retirement income portfolio is one of the most complex retirement planning tasks. Now that you've learned the essential elements of the *Spend Safely Strategy*, you're well on your way to creating a portfolio of retirement income that works for you! You're joining the growing group of older workers who are taking charge of their retirement security.

KEY TAKEAWAYS

▶ If you've covered most of your basic living expenses with Social Security and other sources of guaranteed retirement income, consider taking calculated risks by investing a portion of your savings in stocks.

▶ Investing in stocks provides you with the potential to grow your savings and retirement income over the course of your retirement. Understand that there's the risk that the stocks you've invested in will go down from time to time, but that's the potential price you'll pay for the possibility to significantly grow your retirement bonus.

▶ Simple, effective ways to invest in stocks include low-cost target date funds, balanced funds, and stock index funds.

Refinements and Adjustments to Personalize the Strategy

The three steps of the *Spend Safely Strategy* described in Section 1 include simple, powerful strategies that can help you generate retirement income for the rest of your life. Many people, however, might want to refine and adjust the *Spend Safely Strategy* to meet their specific goals and circumstances. This section describes several straightforward refinements that can help you personalize the strategy and make it work better for you. Feel free to pick and choose the chapters that appeal to you most.

Chapter 5

If You Want Additional Retirement Paychecks

Do you want more retirement income that's risk-protected, even after optimizing your Social Security income, as described in Chapter 2? Are you uncomfortable investing a significant portion of your retirement savings in the stock market to generate retirement bonuses?

If boosting your protected income will help you feel more confident, then this chapter is for you. It describes three possible methods for increasing your risk-protected income:

1. Buy an annuity, aka a personal pension.
2. Make careful decisions if you participate in a pension plan.
3. Use a reverse mortgage on your home.

Let's look at each of these methods in more detail.

Consider buying an annuity, aka a personal pension

If you don't participate in a pension plan, then you might consider using a portion of your retirement savings to buy a single premium immediate annuity, or SPIA for short (pronounced "spee-ah") from an insurance company. Purchasing a monthly annuity is like buying a personal pension. Like your Social Security income, annuities are another way to protect against stock market crashes and the risk of living a long time. You can also buy an annuity that helps protect you against inflation by investing in one that periodically increases your monthly check.

With a SPIA, you pay a portion of your retirement savings to an insurance company. It then invests your money and guarantees to pay you a monthly retirement paycheck for the rest of your life, no matter how long you live. The insurance company also guarantees that your monthly income won't drop due to stock market crashes.

The annualized amount of the annuity you'll receive depends on the type of annuity you purchase, as well as your age, sex, and marital status. By choosing a joint-and-survivor annuity, you can elect to have the income continue to your spouse or partner after you die.

You have some choices and flexibility when buying an annuity. For example, you can buy an annuity with a monthly payment that's fixed in dollar amount. Or you can buy an annuity that increases the monthly payment each year at a fixed rate, such as 2%, 3%, or 4%. As mentioned above, such an annuity can help protect you against inflation, but it will cost you more than a fixed annuity.

If you want to preserve the flexibility of your savings during the early part of your retirement, you can wait to buy such an annuity until you're in your 70s or even later. At an older age, income stability and protection against fraud may become more important goals to you than financial flexibility.

> *Overlook the bad rap that annuities sometimes get by shopping for cost-effective annuities without complicated bells and whistles.*

Annuities sometimes get a bad rap as a result of their high transaction costs or pricey bells and whistles. But these are the expensive variety of annuity.

You're usually better off buying a simple SPIA through a competitive and transparent online annuity bidding service, such as Income Solutions, ImmediateAnnuities.com, or SPIA.direct. These annuity bidding platforms search for the best deal among a handful of reputable insurance companies. They don't charge high transaction fees, and because the annuities are simple and straightforward, you don't need to worry about paying for complicated features you don't need. These bidding services will also show you information on the financial stability of the insurance companies you're considering. Some financial institutions, such as Fidelity Investments, Schwab and Vanguard, can also help you buy a cost-effective annuity.

As with any financial product or instrument, there are both good buys and lemons. Be wary of being sold an annuity by an agent who might not have your best interests at heart and instead wants to earn a high commission on your investment. Your job is to do your research and select the annuity that pays you the most retirement income, taking into consideration the strength of the insurance company.

If you're working with an adviser, ask how much in commissions, special bonuses, and perks they'll receive if you buy the annuity they recommend. Again, you want to make sure they're looking for an annuity that generates the most retirement income for you and not the highest compensation for them. To ensure you get what you need at the best possible price, spend as much time doing your homework as you'd spend on any important purchase, such as a car or long vacation.

Some 401(k) plans and other employer-sponsored retirement plans may offer SPIAs that you can purchase through the plan. These annuities often enjoy group pricing that can deliver more retirement income than what you'd get if you bought an annuity on your own. Investigate whether your 401(k) plan offers this feature.

Do you own a whole life insurance policy with significant cash value? This could be another possible source for buying an annuity. Often, these policies let you convert a life insurance policy into an annuity. Using this feature might make sense if you no longer need life insurance—for instance, if your kids are grown and aren't dependent on you, or if your spouse won't need the life insurance proceeds.

As with many decisions you'll have to make regarding your retirement years, SPIAs come with a few downsides. First, they don't return any unused funds to your heirs after you die, unless you purchase a joint-and-survivor annuity, a cash-refund annuity, or a period-certain annuity. You'll want to investigate these features if it's important for you to pass along money to your beneficiaries or heirs.

Second, annuity contracts typically don't let you change your mind and withdraw your savings once you've purchased the annuity. In other words, they aren't liquid.

Here's something else to consider: You might be more comfortable with the lack of liquidity if you've built a sufficient emergency cash stash. It also helps if you don't use *all* your savings to purchase an annuity. Instead, use some of your savings to invest and draw down, as described in Chapters 3 and 4. This way, you'll still have access to that portion of your savings.

Finally, it's important to understand that annuities' lack of liquidity actually has an important advantage: You can't lose your savings due to making mistakes or being defrauded. That's because the insurance company takes care of investing your savings, and it won't release the money for any purpose other than paying your monthly retirement paycheck. You might appreciate this advantage when you reach your 70s and 80s, and you're less willing or able to manage your investments.

If this lack of liquidity still bothers you, you can buy more complex annuities that allow you to change your mind and withdraw your remaining savings at any time, yet still promise you a lifetime monthly benefit. To account for the cost of this flexibility, the annuity company will usually pay a lower monthly benefit compared to that of a SPIA. However, you may feel more comfortable with this type of annuity knowing you can withdraw your funds if you need them.

These more complex annuities go by such names as

"variable annuities" (VAs) or "fixed index annuities" (FIAs). They often feature "guaranteed lifetime withdrawal benefits" (GLWB). These annuities are often sold by insurance agents and come with high commissions, so shop carefully to find the one with the lowest fees and the most favorable terms. For details on these more complex annuities, see my book *Money for Life: Turn Your IRA and 401(k) Into a Lifetime Retirement Paycheck* or some of the other books and websites listed at the end of this book in the "Helpful Resources" section.

Make careful decisions if you participate in a pension plan

If you participate in your employer's defined-benefit pension plan or cash balance plan, then you're lucky, because these plans are becoming increasingly rare. With such a plan, you're eligible to elect a monthly income that's guaranteed to be paid for the rest of your life, no matter how long you live, and won't decrease if the stock market crashes.

> *If you've earned a substantial pension benefit from your employer and the company offers you a lump sum payment instead of a lifetime annuity, resist the temptation to choose the lump sum! It might not be the best choice for you.*

If your employer offers you the option to take your benefits in one lump sum, resist this temptation! It's a trap for the unwary. You'll be converting a guaranteed, lifelong retirement paycheck into a retirement bonus that isn't guaranteed to last for life and isn't protected against investment losses. If you've earned a substantial pension benefit, then deciding between the lump sum and the monthly pension will be one of the most important financial decisions you'll make for your retirement.

To help you decide which would work better for you, you'll want to first estimate the monthly income you'll receive from your plan. Most pension plans have online calculators you can use to estimate the amount of your monthly check once you retire, or you can request an estimate from your plan's administrator.

Next, find out how much retirement income you can reasonably generate if you decide to elect the lump sum and invest it elsewhere. For example, you could see how much of a retirement bonus the lump sum could generate if you used the IRS required minimum distribution to determine your retirement bonus, or if you bought an annuity as described previously in this chapter. Compare these estimates to the amount of income you'll receive if you elect the monthly pension. Having a clearer idea of what you can expect to get in each case should make your decision easier.

For most people, there's a very good chance you'll receive more retirement income over the course of your lifetime if you take the monthly income, compared to investing the lump sum and using a Retirement Income Generator (RIG) to generate retirement income, as described in Chapters 3 and 4. That's because the amount of the lump sum payment is often below the fair market value of the pension, due to the IRS regulations that dictate how plan sponsors must calculate these lump sum payments.

With most pension plans, the monthly retirement income you're earning will grow if:

- you continue working at your employer and earn more service years,
- you get a raise that's reflected in the calculation of your benefits, and/or
- you delay retirement until the plan's "normal retirement age."

Your plan's online calculator or administrator can show you how much your monthly retirement paycheck might increase if you keep working, get a raise, or delay the start of your pension. This information can also help you decide when to retire.

It's important to note that in most cases, your election is irrevocable. So if you choose the lump sum, you permanently forfeit the right to receive a lifetime monthly check. Similarly, if you elect the monthly payment, you can't change your mind and elect a lump sum later.

One last thought: If you're married and decide to go with the monthly payment option, it's usually a good idea to elect a joint-and-survivor annuity that protects your spouse by continuing part or all of your retirement paycheck after you're gone.

Investigate getting a reverse mortgage on your home if you need more guaranteed income

If you have substantial home equity and your financial resources aren't adequate to support your living expenses in retirement, it's definitely a good use of your time to learn more about the potential uses of a reverse mortgage. Let's discuss the basics.

You can tap your home equity through a federal government-insured Home Equity Conversion Mortgage that's available to homeowners age 62 and older; this type of mortgage is most commonly referred to as a "reverse mortgage." Reverse mortgages are loans against home equity that aren't repaid until the owner dies, moves away, or sells the house. The balance of the loan accumulates with interest on the loan proceeds, and the balance is deducted from the net proceeds of the house when it's eventually sold.

The loan proceeds can be paid to you in one lump sum, from time-to-time as needed, or in periodic monthly payments, known as "tenure payments." Such a tenure payment can supplement your Social Security benefits, similar to an annuity. However, unlike Social Security income, tenure payments don't increase with inflation. This payment will be paid as long as you live in the house and keep up with homeowner obligations, such as property taxes, maintenance, and insurance.

Be aware, however, that reverse mortgages have significant upfront costs. These costs are only worth paying if you really need the money to live on during your retirement, if staying in your home is very important to you, and if you plan to stay in your home for 10 years or more after getting the reverse mortgage.

There are several ways you can use reverse mortgages to help secure your retirement, so if this is something you're considering, it would be a good idea to learn more about your options. My recent book, *Retirement Game-Changers*, goes into more detail about reverse mortgages and also identifies helpful resources for further study.

Here's the bottom line for this chapter: Take the time you need to explore all your options for generating additional risk-protected retirement income. Doing your homework will help you sleep better at night and enjoy your retirement.

KEY TAKEAWAYS

▶ If you want more guaranteed lifetime retirement income, consider using a portion of your savings to buy a cost-effective annuity.

▶ If you participate in a traditional pension or cash balance plan, electing the monthly annuity income option—as opposed to taking a lump sum payment—is usually the best way to increase your guaranteed lifetime retirement income.

▶ It may be possible to use your home equity to set up a reverse mortgage that will deliver a monthly tenure payment, which can be paid for as long as you live in your house.

Chapter 6

If You Expect Uneven Living Expenses During Retirement

Implementing the baseline *Spend Safely Strategy* will help you generate a steady flow of income from retirement paychecks and bonuses throughout your retirement. However, you might want to adjust your strategy to account for any additional expenses you anticipate may only last for a limited period during your retirement. The following are a few straightforward strategies you can use to customize the baseline *Spend Safely Strategy* to meet these goals.

Plan for fun

"Enjoy life while you can. You just never know how long you'll be healthy." I hear this statement frequently from my family and friends, who'd like to travel during the initial years of their retirement, while they still have the health and vitality for such activities. If this describes you, you might be wondering how you can spend more money on travel without jeopardizing your long-term financial security.

Here's one solution: Set aside a "travel fun bucket" to cover these anticipated expenses. Be sure to segregate this bucket from the savings you'll use to generate your retirement bonuses as described in Chapter 3, because the savings you use to generate your bonuses should be invested differently from your travel fun bucket.

Note that the funds for this travel fun bucket don't necessarily need to be physically withdrawn from retirement vehicles, such as an IRA or 401(k) plan, in order to separate them from your retirement savings. Instead, you could simply establish this bucket as a separate investment account within an existing IRA or 401(k) plan.

Note also that when withdrawals from 401(k) plans or deductible IRAs are more than the amounts required by the IRS required minimum distribution (RMD) for the calendar year, as described in Chapter 3, there'll be no violations of the RMD rules for that year. The actual RMD amount is just a minimum; you can always withdraw more than the minimum without penalty.

You'll most likely be making withdrawals from your travel fun bucket in the earlier years of your retirement, so the money will have a relatively short investing horizon. Since that's the case, you could invest these funds in short-term bond funds or conservatively invested balanced funds. Any interest and investment earnings on your travel bucket fund can increase your future withdrawals from the travel bucket.

If you're thinking about establishing a travel fun bucket, decide how much money you'll want in it, and set it up before establishing the investment vehicles that will generate your retirement bonuses. Then you can invest your remaining savings to generate your retirement bonuses, as described in Chapter 4.

If you don't end up using all the money in your travel fun bucket, you can always add it back to the savings that are generating retirement bonuses, or use it to replenish your cash stash.

LEARN BY EXAMPLE

How Maria will fund her travel adventures

Maria, a hypothetical woman who is planning ahead for her retirement, wants to spend $5,000 per year on travel during the first 10 years of her retirement. To pay for these anticipated expenses, she sets aside $50,000 ($5,000 multiplied by 10 years) from her savings in a separate travel fun bucket.

In the first year she's retired, Maria spends $5,000 from her travel fun bucket, but at the end of that first year, her travel fun bucket balance is $46,000 due to investment earnings and/or interest. That means, in the second year, she could technically afford to withdraw $5,111 from her travel fun bucket ($46,000 divided by nine years). She could also choose to spend less in some years, giving her more to spend in other years. Another benefit of having her travel money in a separate investment is that Maria will easily be able to see exactly how much travel fun money she can afford to spend before she uses up her travel fund.

Consider strategies to pay off your mortgage

The travel fun bucket method could also be used to fund other living expenses that you expect to be temporary. For example, you may be near the end of a mortgage payment schedule, in which case mortgage payments will stop at a fixed date in the future. In this case, you could set aside a "mortgage payment bucket" to cover these anticipated expenses and segregate this bucket from the savings you're using to generate your retirement bonuses.

As an alternative to setting up a mortgage payment bucket, you could use the same funds to actually pay off the mortgage. There are pros and cons to this approach, depending on the interest rate on your mortgage, whether the mortgage helps reduce your income taxes, and your desire to have savings that you can access. You might want to consult with a financial adviser to help you decide whether to pay off your mortgage.

LEARN BY EXAMPLE

How Larry and Julie will pay off their mortgage

After they retire, hypothetical couple Larry and Julie will have five years of payments left on their mortgage. Their mortgage payment is $1,500 per month, or $18,000 per year. They decide to set aside $90,000 in their mortgage payment bucket ($18,000 multiplied by five years) and don't include that amount in the funds used to generate their retirement bonuses under the *Spend Safely Strategy*.

Because the mortgage payment bucket would have a relatively short investing horizon, the money could be invested in short-term bond funds, money market funds, or stable value funds.

Again, if you don't end up using all the money in your mortgage payment bucket because it increased due to investment earnings and/or interest, you can always add it back to the savings that are generating retirement bonuses, or use it to replenish your cash stash.

Prepare for potentially high costs of medical and frail care

Many baby boomers have helped their parents navigate their final years, and the time and expense involved have been a serious wake-up call for them. While they stepped up to the plate to help their parents, they want to be better prepared for their own final years.

This is another example of uneven expense flows— additional expenses that you expect to have in your later years for out-of-pocket medical expenses or care when you become frail (aka long-term care).

It's possible that you'll be able to pay for some of these expenses from your retirement paychecks and bonuses, and then adjust your budget for living expenses. For example, you might be able to cover the cost of deductibles and copayments for Medicare and your supplemental medical insurance policy.

While you're planning for retirement, develop a strategy to address the threat of potentially high long-term care expenses. If you ignore this essential task, you could become a significant financial burden on your children or other relatives.

But long-term care isn't covered by Medicare or most medical insurance policies. And expenses for long-term care could be large enough to overwhelm your expected retirement paychecks and bonuses. As a result, I highly recommend that you develop a strategy to address the threat of potentially high long-term care expenses.

One way to do this is to set aside some savings dedicated for that purpose, similar to the methods I suggested you implement for a travel fund or for paying off your mortgage. If you decide to do this, you'll want to coordinate with your retirement income strategy, as shown in the next example.

There are a few important things to keep in mind about planning ahead for long-term care expenses:

- It's very difficult to predict what your out-of-pocket expenses for frail care will be, and they could easily exceed the amounts you've set aside for this purpose. Because of this, you'll want to explore additional strategies that can help you address the risk of frail-care expenses, such as buying long-term care insurance, holding your home equity in reserve, arranging for a reverse mortgage line of credit, or buying a qualified longevity annuity contract (QLAC). A QLAC is a fixed lifetime annuity that you buy when you retire but that doesn't start generating monthly income until you've reached an advanced age, such as 80 or 85.

- If the amount you set aside for long-term care expenses is part of a 401(k) plan or deductible IRA, your annual withdrawals are subject to the RMD rules. If you postpone significant withdrawals after the RMD rules apply to you, you might violate the RMD rules and incur substantial penalties. You could use one of two strategies to address this possibility:
  - o Hold these savings in a Roth IRA or Health Savings Account (HSA), both of which aren't subject to the RMD rules.
  - o Withdraw the required minimum amount from your savings, include this amount in your taxable income for the year, and invest the net amount in an after-tax investment account that you set up for this purpose.

- When you retire, the money you set aside for long-term care expenses will most likely have a long investing horizon. Depending on your tolerance for investment risk, this might justify a substantial investment in stocks for the savings you're intending to use to pay for health care costs late in life.

A complete discussion of the strategies you could use to cover the cost of long-term care later in life is beyond the scope of this short book. For more details, please see my recent book, *Retirement Game-Changers: Strategies for a Healthy, Financially Secure, and Fulfilling Long Life.*

How Linda and Phil will pay for the cost of long-term care expenses

To help cover the cost of potential extra medical and frail care expenses in their later years, Linda and Phil, a hypothetical couple looking ahead to their later years, plan to hold their home equity in reserve so it's available to tap in the future if they need it. But they also want to set aside some savings, too, so they segregate $75,000 from the retirement savings they plan to use to generate their retirement bonuses. They have a long investing horizon, since they don't expect to tap into this bucket for at least 15 years. As a result, they invest this bucket significantly in the stock market, with a balanced mutual fund.

Estimate your regular bonuses after making refinements

Once you set aside the buckets described in this chapter, you should estimate the amount of retirement bonuses that your remaining assets can generate. This way, you'll know the regular amount of retirement bonuses that you can expect to get to help pay for your ongoing living expenses.

Let's check in with Linda and Phil to see how this worked out for them.

▼

How Linda and Phil set up the *Spend Safely Strategy*

When they retired, Linda and Phil, the hypothetical couple mentioned previously, had $500,000 in savings. They decided to set aside $50,000 in a travel fun bucket and $75,000 in a medical and frail-care bucket. This left $375,000 in savings to generate their ongoing retirement bonuses.

Both Linda and Phil were 65 when they retired and decided to use the RMD method to calculate their retirement bonuses. In the first year of their retirement, their regular retirement bonus was $11,095 (2.9586% from the 2021 rules in Table 3.1 of Chapter 3, multiplied by $375,000). They're using this amount to supplement their Social Security income in order to cover their ongoing, regular living expenses. In their first year of retirement, they also withdrew $5,000 from their travel fun bucket for travel expenses.

They'll continue drawing down their travel fun bucket and only dip into their medical and frail-care bucket if they need to. If they don't end up using all the money in their medical and frail-care bucket by the time both of them pass away, the money can serve as a legacy for their children or charities. Once Linda and Phil reach age 72 and are subject to the IRS RMD rules, they'll make sure that their total annual withdrawals from all their buckets comply with these rules.

I know I've given you a lot to think about in this chapter, but it's well worth your time to customize the *Spend Safely Strategy* to support the life you want in retirement. And by preparing for late-in-life costs, you'll also help set your mind at ease that you won't be a burden to your children or other relatives.

KEY TAKEAWAYS

▶ If you want to spend extra money on travel during the first years of your retirement, set aside a "travel fun bucket" from the savings you're using to generate your retirement paychecks and bonuses.

▶ You can also use this bucket approach to pay for mortgage payments or to help cover the cost of medical or frail-care expenses later in life.

▶ Estimate the amount of the retirement bonus your remaining savings will generate after you've set aside money for the buckets described in this chapter. Make sure you'll have enough income, together with Social Security and other sources, to cover your ongoing living expenses. If not, you may need to reconsider your "bucket" plans.

Chapter 7

If You'll Work Awhile in Retirement

After you retire from full-time work, you might decide it would be a smart move to work part time for a few more years as part of a "downshifting" strategy. And you'd probably be making the right choice: Working longer can significantly improve your retirement finances because it enables you to delay both starting Social Security and drawing down your retirement savings until a later date, which will significantly increase your retirement income.

If you decide you want to do this, you may want to consider adjusting your strategy for generating your retirement paychecks and bonuses. Let's discuss what changes you might want to make.

Explore downshifting to increase your retirement security

There are several reasons people decide to work part time after they retire from their full-time jobs: They need the money or the health coverage, they like their job, or they enjoy the social contacts and fulfillment they get from work. But one of the smartest reasons to continue working part time is to delay starting your Social Security income and drawing down your retirement savings, a powerful strategy for maximizing your retirement income. (Examples in Chapters 12 and 13 demonstrate the potential benefits of this strategy.)

Suppose, however, that your part-time work earnings aren't enough to cover *all* your living expenses. Whatever you do, don't start Social Security benefits to supplement your work earnings! This can lead to a very common mistake I see retirees make: They begin working part time *and* start their Social Security benefits, then get used to spending at this level of income. But once they're no longer able to work or can't find work, they find themselves in a financial jam.

Instead of starting your Social Security benefits to cover the gap in income needed to pay for your living expenses, use your retirement savings to supplement your earnings from work. You can do this either by implementing your retirement bonus plan or by setting up a Social Security bridge payment.

If your earnings plus your retirement bonus and/or Social Security bridge payment still aren't enough to cover your living expenses, you should revisit your overall retirement strategy. You might also need to find a way to reduce your living expenses, which would be a better choice than starting your Social Security benefits too early.

I acknowledge that modifying your retirement strategy or reducing your living expenses might be tough choices. But I'd rather that you understand and consider these choices *now* instead of waiting until a time in the not-too-distant future when you experience a financial crisis. At that time, you might have more limited options to make things better.

If you're lucky, your earnings from work might be more than the amount you need to cover your living expenses. In this case, you might want to set aside your surplus earnings for the future, perhaps in a bucket that would help pay for medical and frail care in your later years.

Another way to use excess earnings from work is to pay for your travel expenses. If this works out for you, you might not need to set aside a separate travel fun bucket, as described in Chapter 6. You could also use your earnings to help pay off your mortgage, so that you won't need to set aside a mortgage payment bucket after you stop working.

When it comes to funding your retirement, you'll want to be sure to plan ahead for the years when you're no longer able to work even part time.

No matter what you use any part-time earnings for, you'll want to be sure to plan ahead for the time when you're no longer able to work even part time. You can do this by estimating what your Social Security benefits will be when you eventually start receiving them, as well as what your retirement bonus will be at the time you start drawing it from your savings. Make sure that when you eventually retire completely, your total retirement income can cover your living expenses.

Working part time for a temporary period in retirement has other possible advantages, including these:

- It gives you valuable social contacts and a reason for getting up in the morning.
- It might make you eligible for medical insurance, which can help reduce your living expenses, particularly if you retire before age 65, when you're eligible for Medicare.

Of course, working longer can be "easier said than done," particularly during economic downturns. If you want to work in your retirement years, it's wise to take steps now to improve the chances you'll be able to work. My previous book, *Retirement Game-Changers*, devotes an entire chapter to this topic, and the "Helpful Resources" section at the end of this book includes some books that I respect.

Once again, it's well worth your time to find ways to personalize the *Spend Safely Strategy* to your specific situation, including the possibility of working in your retirement years.

KEY TAKEAWAYS

▶ Working longer can significantly increase your eventual retirement income by enabling you to delay starting Social Security and drawing down your retirement savings.

▶ You might also realize other advantages to working awhile during your retirement.

Chapter 8

If You'd Like to Consider Alternative Retirement Income Generators

Many retirees want or need more income in their initial years of retirement than the amount of income they'd get by using the IRS required minimum distribution (RMD) method of generating retirement bonuses described in Chapters 1 and 3. Fortunately, there are alternative Retirement Income Generators (RIGs) you could consider. By producing a different pattern of retirement income over the course of your lifetime, compared to the RMD, another option might be a better choice for you given your particular goals and circumstances. It would be smart to investigate your options.

Decide if it makes sense to use an alternative RIG

One key feature of the RMD is that it tends to "backload" a larger portion of your retirement income to your later years. This means that the amount of retirement income you'd generate in your initial years of retirement when using the

RMD method might be lower than the income produced by other methods. However, the amount of income produced by the RMD is expected to catch up to and eventually surpass the amount of income produced by alternative methods.

Whether you view this feature of the RMD as an advantage or disadvantage depends on your preferences and situation. There are definitely circumstances in which you might want to personalize your RIG to better meet your own goals and situation, and some methods you might use for that task.

Before you can decide if an alternative RIG would work better for you, however, you'll want to estimate how much your retirement income would be if you used the RMD method. If you discover that the amount of this income will be small, which will likely be the case if you have retirement savings of $200,000 or less, it might not be worth the trouble to search for and use an alternative RIG, since it might not produce a noticeable difference in the amount of your *total* retirement income.

> *When considering alternative RIGs, think about whether the difference in retirement income will significantly improve your life in retirement. Most other RIGs are more complicated to implement or manage, compared to using the RMD. Consider if the trouble of using a different RIG is worth your time to investigate.*

But if you've determined that it would be worth the trouble to refine your RIG because the money generated from a different method is essential, then you have two options:

- You can accelerate your income to the initial years of your retirement, when you think you might be more vital and able to enjoy the additional income.
- You can defer income to the later years of your retirement, when you think you might need more income to pay for higher medical and frail-care costs.

Keep reading to learn how each of these options works.

Consider adjusting your RIG to accelerate income to the earlier part of your retirement

First, note that setting up a "travel fun bucket" or "mortgage payment bucket," as described in Chapter 6, are two straightforward ways to accelerate income to the initial years of your retirement. If either of those options seems like a good fit for you, you can set up one or both of them and then you may not need to change the RIG for your remaining savings if your goal was to increase the amount of money you have available early on.

There's another straightforward way to achieve the goal of having more money to spend in the early years of your retirement while still using the RMD method to calculate your annual retirement bonus. In this case, you can simply increase your annual retirement bonus by multiplying the annual RMD payment by a fixed percentage, such as 25% or 50%.

For instance, suppose you're age 72, with $200,000 in retirement savings that you're devoting to your RIG. At age 72, under the 2021 rules shown in Table 3.1 of Chapter 3, the RMD withdrawal percentage is 3.6630%, which would mean your annual withdrawal under the RMD would be $7,326. If you increase that amount by 25%, the result would be $9,158, or 1.25 times $7,326. And if you increase the amount by 50%, the result would be $10,989, or 1.5 times $7,326.

While increasing your retirement bonus this way will translate to additional retirement income in your late 60s and 70s, you run the risk of a declining retirement bonus in your 80s and beyond if you don't earn favorable investment returns. If you're interested in a detailed discussion of various possible increases in the RMD withdrawal amount and the interaction with your investment strategy, see Section 6 of the research report titled "Viability of the Spend Safely in Retirement Strategy," which is identified in the "Helpful Resources" section at the back of this book.

Here's one more straightforward way to accelerate income into the earlier years of your retirement: Use a withdrawal percentage that's the greater of the RMD withdrawal percentage and another specified percentage, such as 4%, 5%, or 6%.

For example, suppose, in the previous example, that you adopt a strategy to calculate your retirement bonus by applying the greater of 5% and the RMD percentage to your savings. In this case, 5% of $200,000 is $10,000, which is greater than the RMD withdrawal amount of $7,326. Given this strategy, you could spend $10,000 over the course of the year. At age 81, the RMD withdrawal percentage exceeds 5%, and your strategy for determining your retirement bonus going forward would simply default to the RMD (see Table 3.1 for more details).

Note that in either of the above cases, increasing your retirement bonus to more than the RMD won't result in violating the RMD rules, since in either case, you'd be withdrawing more than the minimum required from your savings.

Here's one catch to adjusting the RMD payment: There's a very good chance that many IRA and 401(k) administrators won't be able to calculate an adjustment to the RMD payment for you. In that case, each year, you'll need to calculate the dollar amount of the withdrawal you want for the year and then inform your IRA or 401(k) administrator of your election. For this purpose, you could ask your IRA or 401(k) administrator to calculate the actual RMD amount for you, and then you'd calculate the adjusted amount.

Explore using alternative RIGs

Instead of investing all your savings and drawing it down using the RMD method, you could also buy an annuity with a portion of your retirement savings, as discussed in Chapter 5. Annuities typically accelerate your income into the earlier years of your retirement, compared to using the RMD method.

One benefit to buying an annuity: They're deemed to automatically comply with the IRS RMD rules for the portion of your savings that are applied to the annuity.

For an analysis and comparison of the patterns of income that various annuities and systematic withdrawal plans (SWPs) might generate for you, see Section 7 of the research report titled "Viability of the Spend Safely in Retirement Strategy," which is identified in the "Helpful Resources" section at the back of this book.

Other possible RIGs that might increase your income in the early years of your retirement include investing in real estate for rental income, or starting your own business. While these can be effective ways to supplement your retirement income, you might eventually reach an age when you no longer want to maintain these investments. Describing these strategies for generating retirement income is beyond the scope of this book.

Investigate deferring retirement income to your later years

The RMD method already tends to defer retirement income to your later years, so if deferring retirement income is an appropriate goal for you, you may be satisfied with the results you'll get from the RMD.

If you're looking to defer more income, however, another straightforward way to defer retirement income into your later years is to withdraw just the interest and dividends earned by your investments. By doing so, you keep the principal intact, preserving your retirement savings for your later years or so you can leave a legacy. This method offers some flexibility: In future years, if you need more retirement income, you can always change your withdrawal method and withdraw more than just your investment earnings.

Note that withdrawing just your investment earnings can work for any retirement savings that isn't subject to the RMD rules, such as savings you have in:

- A Roth IRA,
- A deductible IRA or any 401(k) plan before the RMD rules apply to you,

- A Health Savings Account (HSA), or
- An after-tax account with no special tax advantages.

When the IRS RMD rules apply to you, if you withdraw just your investment earnings, there's a good chance you'll violate those rules by not withdrawing enough money. In this case, you'll want to withdraw the minimum required amount, add that amount to the taxable income you report on your tax return for the year, and invest any part of the withdrawal that you don't spend in an after-tax investment account.

For a comparison of the amount of retirement income you might be able to generate in the first year of your retirement under various RIGs, including a few types of annuities and systematic withdrawal methods, please see the *Retirement Income Scorecard* on the "Bonus Chapters" page of www.restoflife.com. By perusing the scorecard, you'll see that by using some alternative RIGs, the amount of income in the first year of retirement can be up to twice as large as the amount using the RMD methodology. However, this is another example of the "pay me now or pay me later" issue you face with your retirement savings. (See Chapter 3 for more information on the "pay me now or pay me later" topic.) In your later years of retirement, the amount of income you'll generate using the RMD methodology will often catch up and surpass the amounts you might be able to withdraw with some alternative RIGs.

As you can see, there can be a few moving parts to the puzzle of developing a RIG that best meets your goals and circumstances. Keep in mind that you lose some of the simplicity of the *Spend Safely Strategy* if you make significant modifications. However, that could be a trade-off you're willing to make to have the income you need when you need it.

KEY TAKEAWAYS

▶ There are alternative Retirement Income Generators (RIGs) you can use—instead of the baseline required minimum distribution (RMD) approach—that produce different patterns of retirement income over the course of your life. For example, you may want to accelerate income to your early years of retirement or defer it to your later years.

▶ Before you choose a different or modified RIG, estimate the amount of income you'd receive under the RMD method when you retire.

▶ See if the difference in retirement income from any of these alternative RIGs, compared to the RMD, will improve your life in retirement. This process can help you decide if it's worth the trouble to consider an alternative RIG.

Chapter 9

If You're in Poor Health

If you're in poor health and are interested in adjusting your retirement plans to reflect your health concerns, then this chapter helps address your situation.

The baseline *Spend Safely in Retirement Strategy* includes two key steps:

1. Optimize Social Security by delaying the start of benefits.
2. Use the IRS required minimum distribution (RMD) to determine the amount of retirement bonuses you'll generate from your savings. This Retirement Income Generator (RIG) method tends to "backload" retirement income to your later years.

If you're concerned you might not live longer than the averages because of your poor health, you may be hesitant to adopt one or both of these steps—you might not want to plan too far ahead and instead enjoy your retirement "while you still can." While this is a reasonable concern, what you do with this concern could depend on how you define "poor health."

Explore adjustments if you're moderately unhealthy

Suppose you're somewhat overweight, have a few ailments that you're monitoring (like many of us in our 60s or older), or have a family history of chronic diseases. Suppose also that you *don't* have a specific diagnosis for a life-shortening disease, such as heart disease, cancer, diabetes, etc. and that you also haven't smoked for a lifetime. For the purpose of this chapter, I'm calling these circumstances "moderately unhealthy."

For most people, even those who are moderately unhealthy as defined above, delaying the start of Social Security benefits as long as possible (but not past age 70) is such a powerful financial strategy that it still makes sense. The research report "Viability of the Spend Safely in Retirement Strategy," which is identified in the "Helpful Resources" section at the back of this book, provides analyses that support this conclusion.

Delaying the start of Social Security benefits is such a powerful financial strategy that it still makes sense for most people who are only moderately unhealthy.

I realize that if you fit the circumstances described in this chapter, you might not want to delay Social Security benefits all the way to age 70. In that case, you'll still realize a significant financial advantage by delaying Social Security to your

Social Security full retirement age (typically between ages 66 and 67) or to your late 60s, a compromise strategy that could work to your benefit.

For your RIG, it still makes sense to use a version of the IRS RMD method to calculate your retirement bonuses. A key advantage of this method is that it delivers retirement income for the rest of your life, no matter how long you live.

However, you might want to use one of the refinements discussed in Chapter 8 that accelerate retirement income to the initial years of your retirement. Doing so might give you more income to enjoy life while you still can but also help you feel safe that your money will last the rest of your life. After all, you never know—you might end up living a long time!

Understand how to plan if you're diagnosed with a life-shortening disease

Suppose you've been given a diagnosis of a serious, life-shortening disease, such as heart disease, cancer, or diabetes. Or suppose that you've smoked all your life. This situation might call for making significant changes to the *Spend Safely Strategy*.

Whatever you do, don't fall into the second camp of people I described in Chapter 1. These are the people who use their savings like a checking account, spending that money on living expenses as they come due. Often, these people spend their savings at an unsustainable rate and justify it because of their health condition.

Why shouldn't you start spending money as quickly as you'd like? I've seen situations where people with various ailments or diagnoses get motivated to take better care of their health and then end up living a long time! No matter how dire you might think the situation is, you should still set up a retirement income portfolio of guaranteed retirement paychecks and variable retirement bonuses so your money lasts for as long as you need it.

To do that, you could adopt some of the suggestions described earlier in this chapter for moderately unhealthy people. Or this could be an appropriate time to work with a qualified retirement planner who can customize a strategy to meet your goals and circumstances.

As you plan for your future, you'll also want to make sure that your spouse or partner will be secure if he or she outlives you. It's entirely possible that your significant other could live for 10 years or more after you pass away. And if you're in poor health but your spouse is in average or better health, the baseline *Spend Safely Strategy* might still be appropriate for both of you.

In particular, you'll want to make sure that your spouse or partner has enough savings to continue his or her retirement income after you're gone and that your retirement savings aren't drained away by medical bills. One helpful strategy is to increase your cash stash to anticipate high out-of-pocket medical bills.

The bottom line is, you just don't know how long you'll live, so plan for prospering if you and your spouse or partner should live a long time.

KEY TAKEAWAYS

▶ If you're moderately unhealthy, you might want to consider adjusting your retirement income strategy using methods described in previous chapters. But you still want to make sure your retirement income will last for the rest of your life.

▶ When you set aside your cash stash, consider that you may have high out-of-pocket expenses for medical bills, and set aside a higher amount.

▶ If you've been diagnosed with a life-shortening illness, you might want to either adjust your strategy on your own or work with a qualified retirement planner to help you adapt your strategy to your circumstances.

Chapter 10

If You Want to Help Your Children or Give to Charity

As people age, they often think about what they want to do with the money they've been putting away for their later years. Some people want to be able to help their adult children and families now by giving them money when they need it. Others want to donate money to their favorite causes.

The challenge is to determine how to help your family members or donate to charities without jeopardizing your own financial security. After all, if you give away too much money now and later become broke, you might need to move in with your kids! A smarter move is to adopt a strategy for giving money to those who might need it while still protecting your financial security.

This chapter discusses two simple ways to responsibly manage your giving while you're alive: by budgeting for it and by giving a one-time donation. It also discusses how your goals to leave a legacy after you're gone can influence the choice of your retirement income strategy while you're alive.

Budget your giving

Once you set up your retirement paychecks and bonuses, you should have a good idea of the total amount of your retirement income. At this point, you can see if this income covers your expected living expenses and if there's any left over. If there is, you can begin to determine just how much you can afford to give away and to whom.

The most straightforward way to give to children or charities is simply to budget the amount of this help as a part of your regular monthly, quarterly or annual living expenses that's covered by your retirement paychecks and bonuses. Simply tell yourself, your children, and any charities you're donating to that this amount is all you can give without jeopardizing your financial security. I'm sure they'll understand.

Plan for one-time giving

In some situations, it might not be practical to budget for regular financial donations to children or charities. For example, your adult children might need a single lump sum of money because they need help with a down payment on a house. So, how can you decide if you can afford to help them?

If you want to give your children a large monetary gift to help them with a sizable expense, first determine how much that gift will reduce your lifetime retirement paychecks and bonuses.

You should estimate how much your annual retirement income will be reduced if you give them a lump sum. That will help you decide if your retirement savings, after being reduced by the amount of that gift, will still generate enough money to cover your living expenses.

L E A R N   B Y   E X A M P L E

▼

How Bill and Eileen's retirement bonus would be affected by a monetary gift to their son

Bill and Eileen, a hypothetical couple who are both age 75, have a retirement savings balance of $400,000. According to the 2021 rules in Table 3.1, their annual retirement bonus using the RMD method at age 75 will be 4.0650% of their savings, or $16,260.

They've decided they want to give $50,000 to their son and daughter-in-law to help them with a down payment on a house. Can Bill and Eileen afford to do that?

In this case, after making the gift, they'd have $350,000 in savings remaining to generate their retirement bonus. This amount produces an annual retirement bonus of about $14,228, using the RMD methodology at age 75. This represents a reduction of about $2,033 in the first year after they give away $50,000, or $169 per month. The amount of reductions in future years will depend on the investment return on their savings, but it would be in the ballpark of the first-year reduction amount. This analysis roughly estimates the annual amount of Bill and Eileen's lifetime retirement bonus they'll have to forgo each year for the rest of their lives as a result of making this gift.

Now that they know how much the monetary gift will reduce their annual retirement bonus, Bill and Eileen will need to consider if they can still meet their expected living expenses. To offset this reduction, one option would be to set up the financial help as a loan with a repayment schedule instead of as an outright gift.

Understand how planning for a legacy can influence your retirement income strategy

If leaving a financial legacy after you pass on is important to you, this goal can influence your choice of a strategy for generating retirement income while you're still alive. In this case, you might prefer a Retirement Income Generator (RIG) that defers income to your later years, as described in Chapter 8. You'd pay yourself later rather than sooner and potentially have more to leave as a legacy. You could also just live on the interest and dividends generated by your savings, preserving the principal for the legacy. Just make sure that the income generated under either of these methods is enough to cover your basic and discretionary living expenses.

Giving to children or charities can be a compelling goal for older Americans, particularly if you have a strong desire to help the next generation and give back. But you'll want to balance this natural human tendency with your own financial security. I'm sure you'll figure out how to do that.

And now we've covered the refinements and adjustments that can help you personalize the retirement income strategy that best fits your situation. For many people, that's all the information they need to create a retirement income strategy that works for them.

If, however, after reading Chapters 5 through 10, you find that you need more sophisticated refinements than those described in this book, it could be worth your time and effort to work with a retirement adviser who's trained in the complexities of generating retirement income.

For those of you who want to dig a little deeper into the details of the *Spend Safely Strategy*, continue on to Section 3, where you'll find more information.

KEY TAKEAWAYS

▶ You can budget for helping your children and giving to charity as an ongoing living expense— much like a car payment—to be paid from your retirement paychecks and bonuses.

▶ If you want to make a large one-time gift from your savings, estimate the amount that your retirement income will drop as a result of the gift, so you can see if you will still be able to cover your living expenses with the remaining balance.

▶ If you want to leave a financial legacy when you're gone, that goal can influence the strategy you choose to generate retirement income while you're alive.

Advanced Study to Further Your Understanding

The three chapters in this section provide more insights to help you make informed decisions that could significantly improve your financial security in retirement:

- Chapter 11 discusses ideas for managing your income taxes, which will be reduced significantly for most people when they retire.

- Chapter 12 provides more examples of the *Spend Safely Strategy* to help you understand the baseline strategy and a few refinements you can use to personalize the strategy.

- Chapter 13 includes two examples that show how delaying your retirement, even for a few years, can significantly increase your retirement income.

The examples in Chapters 12 and 13 can help you make some important retirement decisions, such as when to retire and how to deploy your retirement savings to best meet your goals and circumstances.

If you get bogged down, set the book aside for a while and go do something fun. You might find it easier to work through the examples after you take a break.

Chapter 11

Tax Considerations

You've been paying many thousands of dollars in income taxes for 30 to 40 years or more—at last, you can take a break! That's because, when you retire, it's very likely you'll pay significantly lower federal and state income taxes compared to when you were working. Our research has demonstrated that retirees with less than $1 million in savings will pay very little federal income tax in retirement.

We documented this conclusion in our 2017 research report, "Optimizing Retirement Income by Integrating Retirement Plans, IRAs, and Home Equity," which you'll find identified in the "Helpful Resources" section of this book. The hypothetical retirees shown in that report were typically paying federal income taxes at a 10% or 15% rate under the income tax rates in effect for 2017 before the 2018 tax reductions went into effect. Due to the reduced tax rates and increased standard deductions from the 2018 tax changes, future retirees will most likely pay even less federal income tax.

Also, don't forget that if you're fully retired and not earning any wages or self-employment income, you won't be paying FICA taxes or any state payroll taxes, such as taxes for unemployment or disability.

As a result of your expected low tax payments, you should make any strategy to manage or reduce your income taxes a secondary objective in relation to other important goals, such as maximizing your lifetime retirement income and maximizing the amount of savings you can access throughout your retirement.

Budget for your income taxes in retirement

Even if you're expecting to pay lower income taxes after you retire, you'll still want to estimate the total amount of income taxes you can anticipate having to pay in retirement. Base this estimate on the amount of income you'll receive from the total of:

- The taxable portion of your Social Security benefits,
- Any Social Security bridge payments you might be paying yourself from your savings (as discussed in Chapter 2),
- Withdrawals from your retirement savings,
- Any pension or annuity income you'll receive, and
- Any income you might earn from working.

It's important to note that a portion of your Social Security benefits won't be included in your taxable income, which will help reduce the income taxes you'll pay. The portion that's exempt from income taxes can range from 15% for the most affluent retirees to 100% for retirees with very low incomes. Many middle-income retirees might only be taxed on less than half of their Social Security benefits.

Remember that any withdrawals you make from deductible 401(k) and IRA accounts will now be included in your taxable income, since this money was considered pre-tax income when it was deposited in your accounts. This means you may have to pay some income taxes on these withdrawals when you file your tax returns each year.

Be sure to budget for income taxes that will be due on withdrawals from your deductible 401(k) and IRA accounts. You can't spend all the money you withdraw.

As a result, you can't really spend *all* of the money you withdraw from these accounts on your living expenses. To manage your cash flow, you might want to set aside a small portion of your withdrawals so you have cash available if you end up owing any taxes when you file your tax returns. You may also want to set up estimated quarterly tax payments or withholding to help pay for income taxes that apply to your taxable withdrawals from savings and any income from working.

Note that withdrawals from a *Roth* IRA or a *Roth* 401(k) account won't be included in your taxable income, since the money in these accounts is post-tax money. That also means you get to keep all the money you withdraw from these accounts.

If you work with a tax accountant, ask him or her to estimate the income taxes you can expect to pay, based on the estimates you've developed, for all the components of your retirement income. Include Social Security, withdrawals from savings, any pension or annuity income you receive, and any income from working.

If you prepare your own taxes with tax preparation software, it should be fairly straightforward for you to estimate the taxes you'll pay in retirement. Tax accountants and tax preparation software should both be able to consider all the various tax rules when preparing these estimates.

Consider the tax advantages of a Social Security bridge payment

If you decide to set up a Social Security bridge payment from your deductible IRA, 401(k), 403(b), or 457 account, as described in Chapter 2, you'll enjoy some income tax advantages.

As mentioned previously in this chapter, a portion of your Social Security benefits won't be subject to income taxes. And by increasing your Social Security income by delaying the start of your benefits with a Social Security bridge payment, you'll increase the amount of your retirement income that won't be subject to income taxes.

Here's why: The IRS determines the portion of your Social Security benefits that is subject to income taxes based on your total taxable income for the year. This includes taxable withdrawals from the retirement accounts mentioned above. If you spend down these retirement accounts by using a Social Security bridge payment, then once you start receiving your actual Social Security benefits, you'll have lower withdrawal amounts paid from these taxable accounts. This reduces the total taxable income that the IRS will use to determine the portion of your actual Social Security benefits that is taxed.

This means you increase the portion of Social Security benefits not included in your taxable income, thereby reducing the future income taxes that you'll pay.

In addition, to help reduce the portion of your Social Security benefits that's subject to federal income taxes, you could also consider converting some or all of your deductible IRA, 401(k), 403(b), or 457 accounts to Roth accounts before you start your Social Security benefits. Such a transaction will trigger immediate income taxes on the amount you convert, however, so you'll want to proceed carefully with this possibility.

If you want to learn more about the tax rules that apply to you in retirement, including the federal income tax rules that apply to Social Security and the IRS required minimum distribution, see the bonus chapter *Navigate the Tax Rules* on the "Bonus Chapters" page of www.restoflife.com.

The bottom line is this: While it's important to keep the tax rules in perspective when it comes to retirement planning, your top priority should still be to maximize your retirement income, given the amount of savings you can access throughout your retirement. Once you've maximized your retirement income, *then* you can consider strategies to manage your income taxes. It's well worth your time to ensure you get the most after-tax *total* income from all your sources of retirement income.

KEY TAKEAWAYS

▶ Most middle-income retirees will pay low federal income taxes.

▶ As a result, your top priority should be maximizing your retirement income and then considering strategies to manage your taxes.

▶ A Social Security bridge payment can deliver tax advantages in addition to helping maximize your risk-protected retirement income.

Chapter 12

Examples of the *Spend Safely in Retirement Strategy*

To help you more clearly understand how the *Spend Safely Strategy* works, this chapter shares two hypothetical examples and a few basic refinements to show you some of your options when it comes to developing your retirement income strategy.

Both examples illustrate how you can potentially increase your total annual retirement income by thousands of dollars by using your savings to fund a Social Security bridge payment. With this strategy, you set aside a portion of your retirement savings to help maximize your lifetime Social Security payout by delaying the start of your benefits.

The examples also show that for many people, a very large portion of their total retirement income will be delivered by Social Security income, which is protected from longevity risk, stock market risk, and inflation risk. Only a small portion of your total retirement income will be generated as a "retirement bonus," which will be subject to these risks, depending on how you invest your savings.

Joan, a hypothetical single woman who plans to retire at age 65, is the focus of the first example. Her example illustrates the potential increase in retirement income that results from working for a few years after leaving a full-time job, even if that employment is only part time.

The second hypothetical example profiles a married couple, Jack and Mary, who both plan to retire at age 65. Their example illustrates in more detail how a travel fun bucket can work. Our 2019 research report, "Viability of the Spend Safely in Retirement Strategy," which is identified in the "Helpful Resources" section at the back of this book, includes similar examples. However, I updated these examples for the proposed RMD rules effective in 2021 regarding the required minimum distributions, as described in Chapter 3.

There are a few graphs and numbers in both of these examples that help illustrate some key concepts, so try to work through them—they'll help you more clearly understand each situation.

See how the Social Security bridge payment can help increase retirement income

Joan is single and plans to retire from her full-time job at age 65 in 2021. Here are the assumptions for Joan's example:

- Her current salary is $50,000 per year.
- In her first year of retirement, Joan can devote $250,000 in retirement savings to her Retirement Income Generator (RIG), after setting aside an emergency fund of $10,000 to cover unexpected expenses, such as home and car repairs, and out-of-pocket medical and dental expenses.

- If she starts receiving Social Security benefits at age 65, her estimated benefit will be $19,476 per year.
- The online Social Security calculator Joan used suggested her optimal strategy would be to delay starting her Social Security benefit until age 70. At that age, her estimated Social Security income would be $27,646 per year, or $8,000 more annually compared to the amount she'd receive if she started her benefits at age 65.

Joan is considering three different retirement scenarios to help her decide whether to work part time for a while and also how to deploy her retirement savings:

- Scenario 1: Retire completely at age 65, and immediately start both Social Security benefits and drawing down savings.

- Scenario 2: Retire completely at age 65, but use a portion of her savings to fund a Social Security bridge payment to enable her to delay taking Social Security benefits until age 70. To do this, Joan would set up her Social Security bridge fund to pay her $27,646 each year between ages 65 and 70. This amount is equal to the annual Social Security benefit she expects to receive if she starts benefits at age 70.

- Scenario 3: Employ a downshifting strategy in which she would work part time between ages 65 and 70. In this option, Joan plans to earn just enough to cover her living expenses so she can delay both starting Social Security and drawing down savings until age 70.

Figure 12.1 shows the annual amount of retirement income that Joan can expect under each of these three scenarios for the first year of her retirement. In future years, her Social Security income will receive cost-of-living increases, and the amount of her future retirement bonuses will depend on the investment return on her savings. In all three scenarios, Joan uses the RMD methodology that would apply in 2021, as described in Chapter 3, to calculate the amount of her retirement bonus.

FIGURE 12.1. Joan's annual retirement income under three scenarios

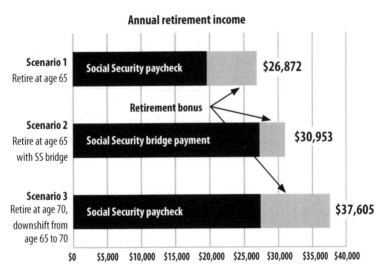

Joan can significantly increase her retirement income with a Social Security bridge payment or by downshifting between ages 65 and 70

Annual retirement income

Scenario	Income
Scenario 1 Retire at age 65	Social Security paycheck — $26,872
Scenario 2 Retire at age 65 with SS bridge	Social Security bridge payment — $30,953
Scenario 3 Retire at age 70, downshift from age 65 to 70	Social Security paycheck — $37,605

Retirement bonus

$0 $5,000 $10,000 $15,000 $20,000 $25,000 $30,000 $35,000 $40,000

With Scenario 2, using the Social Security bridge payment, Joan will increase her total annual retirement income by $4,081 compared with Scenario 1—and under Scenario 2, she still retires completely at age 65.

In Scenario 3, using the downshifting strategy, Joan's total annual retirement income at age 70 would be $10,733 *higher* than the retirement income she would have received using Scenario 1 (starting Social Security benefits and savings drawdown at age 65).

Joan's example illustrates a critical issue she'll need to consider when choosing among the three scenarios described above: that she may need to live on less income, after taxes, when she retires compared to the after-tax income she earned while she was working. This issue is an important planning challenge many older workers face as they approach their retirement years.

Let's dig a bit deeper on this issue. Conventional wisdom often offered by retirement planners is that workers need a total retirement income that's equal to 70% to 80% of their gross income before retirement. This level of retirement income, experts suggest, will help them maintain the same level of after-tax, spendable income they enjoyed while they were working.

But why not try to replace 100% of your gross income before retirement? Following are a few key reasons it's not usually necessary for retirees to replace 100% of their gross pre-retirement income:

- Retirees don't pay FICA and Medicare taxes on Social Security benefits or on withdrawals from retirement savings. (Note, however, if you work part time, you'll pay these taxes on your wages or self-employment earnings.)

- You'll pay significantly lower federal and state income taxes, since a large portion of your Social Security income is exempt from income taxes. In addition, taxpayers age 65-plus enjoy larger tax deductions.
- You no longer need to set aside funds for retirement.

For the above reasons, a gross retirement income that "replaces" 70% to 80% of your pre-retirement gross pay might still deliver approximately the same after-tax, spendable income. But, as you'll see, Joan may still fall short of this 70% to 80% replacement goal.

Figure 12.2 shows that Joan's "replacement rate" only meets this conventional-wisdom goal under Scenario 3, in which she works part time until age 70. In this graph, the bars represent her total retirement income from Social Security and her retirement bonus.

FIGURE 12.2. How much of Joan's salary does her retirement income "replace"?

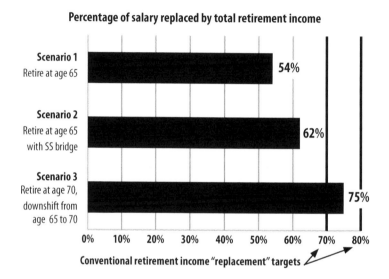

Joan's income falls short of conventional retirement income goals unless she adopts the downshift strategy

Percentage of salary replaced by total retirement income

With this in mind, Joan will have to determine what her estimated living expenses will be during retirement. Once she knows that, she'll be able to more easily decide which scenario might work best for her.

Whether falling short of these conventional-wisdom goals is a problem depends on Joan's goals and circumstances. Joan might decide that she doesn't need as much after-tax, spendable income in retirement, compared to when she was working. For example, she'll no longer have work-related expenses, such as commuting, and she may pay off her mortgage or downsize to a less expensive residence.

Joan might also decide that living on less income is an acceptable price to pay for her retirement freedom and cut back on other expenses to do so.

While Joan doesn't have children, for many other retirees whose children are older and may have moved out, they'll no longer have the expense of paying for their children's living or college expenses.

Joan's analysis also demonstrates the amount of retirement income that's protected from common retirement risks. In Scenarios 1 and 3, more than two-thirds of her income will be risk-protected. With Scenario 2, well over three-fourths of her total retirement income will be risk-protected.

TABLE 12.1. The total percentage of Joan's retirement income that Social Security delivers and is risk-protected

Scenario	Portion of retirement income that's risk-protected	
1. Retire at age 65	72%	
2. Retire at age 65 with Social Security bridge	89%	
3. Downshift between ages 65 and 70	74%	

You can also see this result in Figure 12.1 by comparing the amount of Social Security income Joan will get to the amount of her retirement bonus in each scenario.

See how the travel fun bucket works

Jack and Mary both plan to retire at age 65 in 2021. Here are some relevant assumptions for this hypothetical example:

- Their current annual salaries are $75,000 for Jack and $25,000 for Mary.

- In their first year of retirement, they can devote $400,000 in retirement savings to their RIG, after setting aside an emergency fund of $15,000. This fund will cover unexpected expenses, such as home and car repairs, out-of-pocket medical and dental expenses, and potential financial assistance to family members.

- Jack and Mary consulted an adviser who is trained in optimizing Social Security benefits for retirees. The adviser recommended that the optimal strategy is for Jack to start his Social Security benefits at age 70, while Mary should start her benefits at age 66.

- Here are estimates of Jack's annual Social Security income:
  - If he starts at age 65: $25,344
  - If he starts at age 70: $35,977

- Here are estimates of Mary's annual Social Security income:
  - If she starts at age 65: $12,492
  - If she starts at age 66: $13,406

Jack and Mary are considering three different retirement scenarios to help them decide if they'll need to reduce their living expenses in retirement. They also want to see if they can responsibly spend extra money on travel for the first 10 years of their retirement by using a "travel fun bucket" strategy without jeopardizing their long-term financial security. Using a travel fun bucket will reduce the amount of their ongoing retirement income that's devoted to regular living expenses.

Here are the three scenarios they're considering:

- Scenario 1: Retire at age 65, and immediately start receiving Social Security benefits and drawing down savings.

- Scenario 2: Retire at age 65, and use a portion of their savings to fund a Social Security bridge payment. This will enable Jack to delay his Social Security benefits until age 70 and Mary to delay her benefits until age 66.

- Scenario 3: This scenario is the same as Scenario 2, except they would also create a travel fun bucket to pay for additional travel expenses of $5,000 per year for the first 10 years of their retirement, when they anticipate they'll still be vital and healthy. To do this, they'd reduce the amount of their savings that's generating their RMD retirement bonus by $50,000, which they would set aside to fund their travel fun bucket.

Figure 12.3 shows the annual amount of retirement income that Jack and Mary can expect under each of these three scenarios for the first year of their retirement. In future years, their Social Security income will receive cost-of-living increases, and the amount of their future retirement bonuses will depend on the investment return on their savings. In all three scenarios, they use the RMD methodology that would apply in 2021, as described in Chapter 3, to calculate the amount of their annual retirement bonuses.

FIGURE 12.3. Jack and Mary's annual retirement income under three scenarios

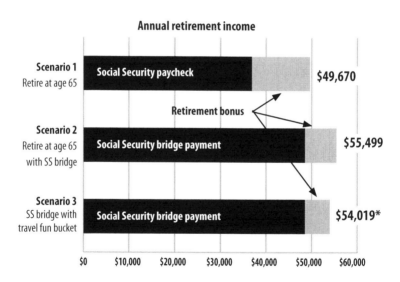

Jack and Mary can significantly increase their ongoing retirement income with a Social Security bridge payment

Annual retirement income

	Annual retirement income
Scenario 1 Retire at age 65	Social Security paycheck — $49,670
Scenario 2 Retire at age 65 with SS bridge	Social Security bridge payment — $55,499
Scenario 3 SS bridge with travel fun bucket	Social Security bridge payment — $54,019*

Retirement bonus

$0 $10,000 $20,000 $30,000 $40,000 $50,000 $60,000

* With Scenario 3, in addition to the income shown in the graph, Jack and Mary will receive $5,000 per year for 10 years to help pay for travel expenses

In Scenario 2, using the Social Security bridge payment, Jack and Mary would increase their total annual retirement income by $5,829 *without* having to change their retirement date.

In Scenario 3, using the travel fun bucket together with the Social Security bridge payment, they'd decrease their ongoing lifetime retirement income by $1,480 per year, compared to Scenario 2, which doesn't include a travel fun bucket. However, compared to Scenario 1, they'd receive $4,349 more annual retirement income. Using the Social Security bridge payment would help "pay" for their travel fun bucket, with money left over. And don't forget: In addition to their ongoing retirement income, Jack and Mary would be able to dedicate an extra $5,000 each year for 10 years specifically to travel expenses.

This analysis should help Jack and Mary more easily decide if they can afford to fund any extra travel in the first 10 years of their retirement without jeopardizing their retirement security for the rest of their lives. They'll also need to consider whether an income of $54,019 per year will be enough to cover their regular, ongoing living expenses.

The bars in Figure 12.4 represent Jack and Mary's total retirement income from Social Security and their retirement bonus. Unfortunately, they show that the couple's "replacement rate" in all three scenarios would fall short of the 70% to 80% amount of gross pre-retirement income that conventional wisdom says people need to "replace."

Jack and Mary are facing the same common retirement planning dilemma that Joan faced: that they may need to live on less after-tax income when they retire compared to when they were working. To address this challenge, Jack and Mary will either need to work longer or reduce their after-tax, spendable income, or explore some combination of these two strategies.

FIGURE 12.4. How much of Jack and Mary's salary does their retirement income "replace"?

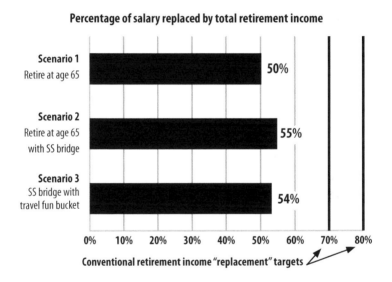

Jack and Mary's income falls short of conventional retirement income goals

Percentage of salary replaced by total retirement income

Scenario 1 Retire at age 65	50%
Scenario 2 Retire at age 65 with SS bridge	55%
Scenario 3 SS bridge with travel fun bucket	54%

0% 10% 20% 30% 40% 50% 60% 70% 80%

Conventional retirement income "replacement" targets

With this in mind, Jack and Mary should take the time to estimate what their living expenses will be during retirement. Once they have a good idea of that, they'll be able to more easily decide which scenario, if any, might work best for them.

The strategy Jack and Mary choose will also impact the portion of their retirement income that's risk-protected.

Table 12.2 shows that the Social Security bridge strategy can increase the portion of their retirement income that's delivered by Social Security, which is protected from common retirement risks, such as living a long time, inflation, and stock market crashes. In Scenario 1, more than three-quarters of their total retirement income is risk-protected. Under Scenarios 2 and 3, an even larger portion of their income is risk-protected.

TABLE 12.2. The total percentage of Jack and Mary's retirement income that Social Security delivers and is risk-protected

Scenario	Portion of retirement income that's risk-protected	
1. Retire at age 65	76%	
2. Retire at age 65 with Social Security bridge	89%	
3. Social Security bridge plus travel fun bucket	91%	

If you'd like to see the details of the math calculations for the two examples in this chapter, please see the bonus chapter titled *Calculation Details of the Spend Safely in Retirement Strategy*, which is available on the "Bonus Chapters" page of www.restoflife.com. Seeing the math might help you better understand the workings of the *Spend Safely in Retirement Strategy*, as well as the refinements.

Congratulations on working through these examples! Both examples illustrate that the *Spend Safely Strategy* is not an inflexible strategy. There are many ways you can customize it to meet your goals and circumstances, making it well worth your time to consider how to personalize the strategy to best fit your situation. Take another well-deserved break, then learn more with the insightful examples in the next chapter.

KEY TAKEAWAYS

▶ You'll have a variety of options available to you when it comes to determining the best financial strategy to employ in your retirement. Be sure to investigate your options before deciding on the one that will work best for you.

▶ The examples in this chapter show how you can potentially increase your total annual retirement income by thousands of dollars with a Social Security bridge payment.

▶ These examples also show how you can responsibly budget for additional travel expenses during the initial years of your retirement.

Chapter 13

The Power of Delaying Retirement

Many older workers think constantly about what the "right" age for them to retire will be. There are many financial and lifestyle factors that go into this critical decision. This chapter drills down on the financial considerations.

Have you considered delaying your retirement past the age at which you had originally planned to leave your full-time job behind? Many people have. So, this chapter offers two hypothetical examples that illustrate the power of delaying your retirement, when your retirement income includes both Social Security benefits and retirement bonuses using the required minimum distribution (RMD) methodology. Both of these examples illustrate the potential significant increase you might gain in retirement income by working for a temporary period during your retirement years, even if such employment is only part time.

Learn how to choose the best age at which to retire from Rob and Betty

Rob and Betty are a middle-income married couple, both age 62, who are trying to determine when it would make the most sense for them to retire from a financial perspective. Rob's current annual salary is $75,000, while Betty's annual earnings are $25,000, for a combined annual household income of $100,000. At this point, they've accumulated $350,000 in retirement savings.

Figure 13.1 shows their retirement income under five different retirement scenarios for the first year of their retirement. In future years, their Social Security income will receive cost-of-living increases, and the amount of their future retirement bonuses will depend on the investment return on their savings. Their retirement income includes both Social Security benefits and retirement bonuses generated from their savings and calculated using the RMD methodology that would apply to 2021 and after, as described in Chapter 3.

Here are the five scenarios illustrated in Figure 13.1:

1. Both Rob and Betty retire completely at age 62 and start receiving Social Security benefits and drawing down retirement savings.
2. Both keep working *part time* until their Social Security Full Retirement Age (66 and 6 months), then both start receiving Social Security benefits and drawing down retirement savings.
3. Both keep working *full time* until their Social Security Full Retirement Age, then both start receiving Social Security benefits and drawing down retirement savings.

4. Both keep working *part time* until age 70, then both start receiving Social Security benefits and drawing down retirement savings.
5. Both keep working *full time* until age 70, then both start receiving Social Security benefits and drawing down retirement savings.

FIGURE 13.1. How delaying retirement significantly increases Rob and Betty's retirement income

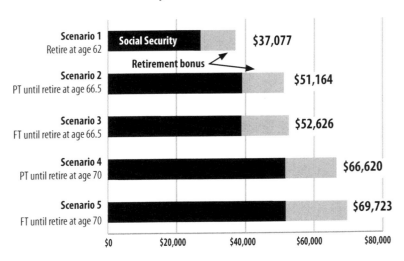

Rob and Betty's annual retirement income

Here are the assumptions made for this hypothetical example:

- Rob and Betty use the IRS RMD to generate their retirement bonus, adjusted for retirements before age 72 as described in Table 3.1.

- The amounts shown are in today's dollars and haven't been adjusted for inflation.
- No future wage increases are taken into account.
- For the part-time working scenarios, Rob and Betty stop contributing to retirement savings.
- For the full-time working scenarios, they contribute 10% of their salary to their retirement savings each year until they retire.
- Savings earn a real rate of return, after adjusting for inflation, of 3% per year.

This example also illustrates the important planning challenge I described earlier in Chapter 12: that Rob and Betty may need to live on less after-tax income in retirement compared to their working years.

Figure 13.2 restates the previous graph shown in Figure 13.1, illustrating how much of Rob and Betty's pre-retirement pay would be "replaced" by their retirement income. The bars represent their total retirement income as a percentage of their pay just before retirement, which includes both Social Security benefits and their retirement bonus.

FIGURE 13.2. Work longer or reduce spendable income?

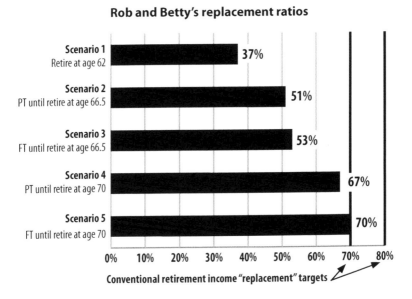

Rob and Betty's replacement ratios

Scenario 1 — Retire at age 62	37%
Scenario 2 — PT until retire at age 66.5	51%
Scenario 3 — FT until retire at age 66.5	53%
Scenario 4 — PT until retire at age 70	67%
Scenario 5 — FT until retire at age 70	70%

Conventional retirement income "replacement" targets

As you can see from the chart above, in every scenario except for Scenarios 4 and 5, Rob and Betty would fall far short of earning the 70% to 80% amount of gross pre-retirement income that conventional wisdom says they'd need to "replace" in retirement, unless they work either part time or full time into their late 60s or 70s. Otherwise, they might need to live on reduced spendable income compared to their working years. Their situation is very typical for many middle-income American workers.

Here are a few more observations we can make from this example:

- Delaying retirement, even if for a few years, can significantly increase the eventual retirement income a person or couple will receive.

- Most of the increase this couple would gain in retirement income comes from delaying both Social Security benefits and savings drawdown; the additional retirement contributions made between age 62 and retirement will only modestly increase the eventual retirement income. This strategy might be a good one for older workers who want more free time but still need the income from working: They can use a downshifting strategy rather than quitting their full-time jobs outright.

- For the scenarios in which Rob and Betty retire before age 70, they don't use a Social Security bridge payment to boost their retirement income. As seen in the examples in Chapter 12, that strategy can provide a significant boost to many people's retirement income.

This type of analysis helps Rob and Betty balance the financial considerations with the other lifestyle factors that will influence their decision about the best age to retire.

Let's look at another example of a couple who have more retirement savings than Rob and Betty and find out how delaying retirement might help them increase their retirement income.

Discover how to choose the best age at which to retire from Rose and Frank

Rose and Frank are married and are both age 60. Rose's current annual salary is $150,000, while Frank's annual earnings are $50,000, giving them a combined annual household income of $200,000. At this point, they've accumulated $1,000,000 in retirement savings.

Figure 13.3 shows Rose and Frank's retirement income under five different retirement scenarios for the first year of their retirement. In future years, their Social Security income will receive cost-of-living increases, and the amount of their future retirement bonuses will depend on the investment return on their savings. Their retirement income includes both Social Security benefits and retirement bonuses generated by their savings and calculated using the RMD methodology.

Here are the five scenarios illustrated in Figure 13.3:

1. Both Rose and Frank work *full time* until age 62, then both retire completely and start receiving Social Security benefits and drawing down retirement savings.

2. Both keep working *part time* until age 65, then both start receiving Social Security and drawing down retirement savings.

3. Both keep working *full time* until age 65, then both start receiving Social Security and drawing down retirement savings.

4. Both keep working *part time* until age 70, then both start receiving Social Security benefits and drawing down retirement savings.

5. Both keep working *full time* until age 70, then both start receiving Social Security benefits and drawing down retirement savings.

FIGURE 13.3. How delaying retirement can significantly increase Rose and Frank's retirement income

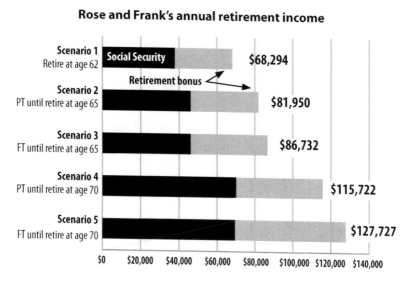

Rose and Frank's annual retirement income

The assumptions for this example are the same as the assumptions for Rob and Betty.

Note that Rose and Frank have a bigger portion of retirement income coming from retirement bonuses compared to Rob and Betty, because they accumulated more in retirement savings. As a result, proportionately less of their income is protected from longevity risk, stock market risk, and inflation risk. Because of this, they might benefit from considering refinements or alternatives to the *Spend Safely Strategy*, as described in Section 2 of this book.

Figure 13.4 restates the graph shown in Figure 13.3 but illustrates how much of Rose and Frank's pre-retirement pay would be "replaced" by their retirement income. The bars represent their total retirement income as a percentage of their pay just before retirement, which includes both Social Security benefits and their retirement bonus. Note that even if they work either full time or part time until age 70, they'd still fall short of the conventional-wisdom replacement goals.

FIGURE 13.4. Work longer or reduce spendable income?

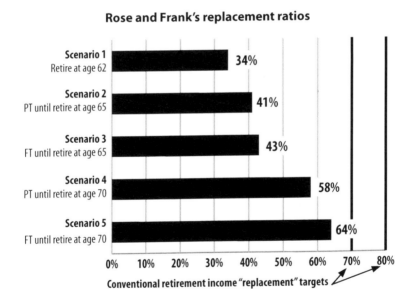

Rose and Frank's replacement ratios

Scenario	Replacement
Scenario 1 Retire at age 62	34%
Scenario 2 PT until retire at age 65	41%
Scenario 3 FT until retire at age 65	43%
Scenario 4 PT until retire at age 70	58%
Scenario 5 FT until retire at age 70	64%

Conventional retirement income "replacement" targets

Here are a few observations we can make from this example:

- As with Rob and Betty, delaying retirement for Rose and Frank would have a significant impact on the total amount of their eventual retirement income.
- Despite the fact that they have more money in retirement savings, Rose and Frank would most likely also fall short of common retirement income targets. Because of this, they'd need to live on less after-tax income compared to when they were working.
- Similar to Rob and Betty, Rose and Frank could significantly boost their retirement income with a Social Security bridge payment for the scenarios in which they retire before age 70.

The analyses shown in these two examples can help you decide when it would make the most sense for you to retire from a financial perspective and whether you should continue working full time or part time until you retire completely. This information can also help you decide if reducing your standard of living is an acceptable price to pay for your retirement freedom. You'll feel much better if you make informed decisions.

While the two analyses in this chapter are for married couples, in my research, I've prepared similar examples for single workers. The results and conclusions are similar to the examples in this chapter.

These analyses also offer a visual picture that can help you decide how much investment risk you'd be comfortable taking with your retirement savings. As I've mentioned before,

Social Security benefits help protect you against longevity risk, inflation risk, and stock market risk, and they'll most likely represent a large portion of your retirement income portfolio. It's only the retirement savings drawdown that's subject to these risks, and that money typically represents a smaller portion of your total retirement income. Assuming investment risk on this smaller portion of retirement income might be an acceptable price to pay for the potential for your savings and retirement bonuses to grow in retirement. But that's a choice you'll have to make for yourself after doing your own analysis.

With that said, it might be difficult for some people to prepare this type of analysis on their own. In that case, it might help to work with a financial adviser who's skilled at preparing this type of retirement income analysis. Such an adviser might also help you prepare an investment strategy for your retirement income portfolio.

Congratulations! You've learned a lot about generating a retirement income that will last the rest of your life, no matter how long you live, and will pay for your living expenses throughout retirement. You'll feel a lot more confident about being able to afford your retirement if you make effective plans that have a good chance of succeeding. These plans can help replace your worry and anxiety about retirement so you can enjoy your retirement years more, knowing that you're not likely to run out of money.

KEY TAKEAWAYS

▶ The examples in this chapter show how you can substantially increase your retirement income by delaying starting Social Security benefits and drawing down your savings, even if only for a few years.

▶ These examples also illustrate how a downshifting strategy can help you more easily achieve these goals.

Resources

To help you apply the *Spend Safely in Retirement Strategy* to your situation, this section includes an easy-to-follow checklist of action steps. It also identifies helpful resources that you can use to learn more about building a portfolio of retirement income, as well as tools that can help you make decisions to plan your retirement.

The *Spend Safely in Retirement Strategy* Action Step Checklist

To help you implement the *Spend Safely Strategy*, here's a step-by-step checklist that summarizes the action steps in this book. Each step might take some time for you to implement, but remember that you don't need to complete it all at once! Work through it at your own pace. It'll be well worth your time.

Prepare by taking inventory

- Find the Social Security estimate that was mailed to your house, or set up a "my Social Security" account at www.ssa.gov.

- Locate statements for all the savings accounts that you can deploy to generate retirement income, such as IRAs, 401(k) accounts, 403(b) accounts, after-tax investments, whole life insurance, etc. Include your spouse or partner's accounts, if you're married or living with a significant other.

- If you have significant money in employer-based savings plan accounts, such as a 401(k) plan or 403(b) plan, then do the following:
  - o Determine if these plans have low-cost investment funds you can use to generate retirement income.
  - o Learn about the options in the plan to generate retirement income, such as monthly installment payments or annuities.
  - o Determine if the plan can pay you the IRS required minimum distribution (RMD).

- If you participate in a traditional pension plan or cash balance plan, locate and read the "Summary Plan Description" that describes your plan. Estimate any monthly income you'll receive. If you're married, adjust for the joint-and-survivor form of payment. Most plans have online systems that will help you prepare these estimates.

- Estimate your living expenses in retirement. These include the following:
  - o Monthly expenses, such as rent or mortgage, food, utilities, car payments, and medical insurance premiums
  - o Periodic expenses, such as insurance payments and property taxes
  - o "Needs" vs. "wants"

- Check to make sure that all your beneficiary designations are up-to-date with any important retirement savings accounts, including your 401(k) plan.

Develop your cash stash

- Estimate the amount of money you'd like to set aside in an emergency fund to help you meet predictable or unpredictable future living expenses that might cost more than your retirement paychecks and bonuses easily cover, such as home or car repairs, out-of-pocket medical bills, dental bills, or financial help for family members. This amount won't be used to generate retirement paychecks or bonuses.

- Select a financial institution where you can invest your cash stash so that you can access it quickly if necessary.

Optimize Social Security

- Estimate your monthly benefits (and those of your spouse if you're married). You can either:
  - o use your written statement, or
  - o use your "my Social Security account" on www.ssa.gov.

- Determine the optimal age at which to start Social Security benefits for yourself and your spouse if you're married. To do this, you can either:
  - o use an online calculator, preferably one that uses your actual wage history, or
  - o work with a financial planner who's trained in optimizing Social Security benefits.

- Develop a strategy to delay Social Security benefits if the optimal age to start is after you retire. To do this, you can either:
  - o use earnings from working, or
  - o set up a Social Security bridge payment fund.

Make the most of your traditional pension plan or cash balance plan

- Determine the best time to start your monthly retirement income by estimating your income under a few different retirement ages. Make sure you use the form of payment that reflects your married status. Include this amount in your guaranteed retirement paychecks.

Generate retirement bonuses

- Decide if you'll set aside buckets for travel fun or mortgage payments, or to pay for medical and/or frail care.

- Estimate the amount of savings you have available to deploy your ongoing retirement bonuses. Here's how to do this:
  - o Subtract the amount needed to fund a Social Security bridge payment, if applicable.
  - o Subtract any amounts for adjustments and refinements, such as buckets for travel fun, mortgage payments, or medical and frail care.
- To calculate the amount of your retirement bonus each year, determine if you'll use the IRS RMD

method without adjustments or whether you'll make adjustments to accelerate income to the early years of your retirement or delay income to your later years. Estimate the amount of your annual retirement bonus.

- Look at the investment funds in your 401(k) plan to determine if the plan offers low-cost funds that can be appropriate for generating retirement bonuses. Also see if your plan can pay installment payments to help you implement your retirement bonus strategy. If it can't, you may need to find a more supportive financial institution and roll your account into an IRA.

- Determine how much of your savings you'll want to invest in the stock market, and select the investment fund(s) you can use to deploy your strategy.

Make refinements, if necessary

- After considering your optimized Social Security benefits and any pension benefits, determine whether you want more risk-protected retirement paychecks. If you do, decide how you'll generate these paychecks, either with an annuity purchase or a tenure payment from a reverse mortgage.

- Determine whether you want to make any adjustments for anticipated uneven living expenses or salary earnings for a temporary period.

Manage your income taxes

- Once you have estimates of all your sources of retire-ment paychecks and bonuses, estimate the federal and state income taxes you might pay during retirement. You can do this by:
    - working with your tax preparer, or
    - using tax preparation software.

- Build these estimates into your budget for living expenses.
- To help you pay your income taxes that are due when you file your tax return, consider setting up quarterly estimated tax payments or withholding.

Answer one more critical question

Now that you've taken these action steps, you have one more question to ask yourself: Do your estimated retirement paychecks and bonuses cover your expected living expenses?

If yes, you have a feasible plan to generate retirement income throughout your life!

If no, you might need to adjust your plan by:

- working longer,
- reducing your spending, or
- doing some combination of the two.

Don't worry—plan and be happy! I know it's been a lot of effort to plan for a financially secure retirement, but now you're prepared. It's time to celebrate, so go do something fun to reward yourself for your hard work!

Helpful Resources

Bonus chapters on the "Bonus Chapters" page of www.restoflife.com

- Calculation Details of the *Spend Safely in Retirement Strategy*
- Get Help
- Navigate the Tax Rules
- Retirement Income Scorecard
- Stock Investing in Retirement—Opportunity and Risk

Online annuity bidding platforms

- ImmediateAnnuities.com: www.immediateannuities.com
- Income Solutions: www.incomesolutions.com
- SPIA.direct: www.spia.direct

Research and studies on retirement income strategies

We conducted the following studies at the Stanford Center on Longevity, in collaboration with the Society of Actuaries. The two most recent reports analyzed the *Spend Safely in Retirement Strategy* in detail. These reports are on the publications page of the Stanford Center on Longevity: http://longevity.stanford.edu/#publications

- Pfau, Wade, Tomlinson, Joe, and Vernon, Steve. "Viability of the Spend Safely in Retirement Strategy." *Stanford Center on Longevity*. May 2019.
- Pfau, Wade, Tomlinson, Joe, and Vernon, Steve. "Optimizing Retirement Income by Integrating Retirement Plans, IRAs, and Home Equity: A Framework for Evaluating Retirement Income Decisions." *Stanford Center on Longevity*. November 2017.
- Pfau, Wade, Tomlinson, Joe, and Vernon, Steve. "Optimizing Retirement Income Solutions in Defined Contribution Retirement Plans: A Framework for Building Retirement Income Portfolios." *Stanford Center on Longevity*. May 2016.
- Vernon, Steve. "The Next Evolution in Defined Contribution Retirement Plan Design: A Guide for DC Plan Sponsors to Implementing Retirement Income Programs." *Stanford Center on Longevity*. September 2013.

Retirement planning books

Here are books that cover a range of retirement planning topics, and some that specialize in retirement income strategies:

- *Great Jobs for Everyone 50+: Finding Work That Keeps You Happy and Healthy ... and Pays the Bills*, by Kerry Hannon. Wiley, 2017.

- *How a Second Grader Beats Wall Street: Golden Rules Any Investor Can Learn,* by Allan Roth. Wiley, 2009.

- *How Much Can I Spend in Retirement?: A Guide to Investment-Based Retirement Income Strategies,* by Wade Pfau, Ph.D. Retirement Researcher Media, 2017.

- *How to Make Your Money Last: The Indispensable Retirement Guide,* by Jane Bryant Quinn. Simon & Schuster, 2020.

- *Money for Life: Turn Your IRA and 401(k) Into a Lifetime Retirement Paycheck,* by Steve Vernon, FSA. *Rest-of-Life* Communications, 2012.

- *Never Too Old to Get Rich: The Entrepreneur's Guide to Starting a Business Mid-Life,* by Kerry Hannon. Wiley, 2019.

- *Retirement Game-Changers: Strategies for a Healthy, Financially Secure, and Fulfilling Long Life,* by Steve Vernon, FSA. *Rest-of-Life* Communications, 2018.

- *Safety-First Retirement Planning: An Integrated Approach for a Worry-Free Retirement,* by Wade Pfau, Ph.D. Retirement Researcher Media, 2019.

Retirement planning websites with a focus on retirement income

Here I identify a number of helpful websites. It's not practical to provide the exact URL, but you can find these sites by searching for the name and topic.

- IRS required minimum distribution:
  - AARP
  - Financial Industry Regulatory Authority (FINRA)
  - IRS website
  - Many financial institutions and 401(k) administrators also have online RMD calculators and resources.

- *How Much Can I Afford to Spend in Retirement?* This website is maintained by retirement researcher and actuary Ken Steiner, FSA, and contains several articles on generating retirement income to meet your spending needs. It also contains a calculator to help you determine appropriate withdrawals from savings.

- *Managing Retirement Decisions,* maintained by the Society of Actuaries:

  - "Designing a Monthly Paycheck for Retirement"
  - "Lump Sum or Monthly Pension: Which to Take?"

- *Morningstar.* An online service that rates a variety of investments, including mutual funds, and provides a wealth of descriptive briefs and blog posts.

- *National Resource Center on Women and Retirement Planning.* This website contains useful tools and resources with a special focus on the issues that are important for women.

- *NewRetirement.* This website contains useful tools and articles for developing a retirement income portfolio.

- *Retirement Researcher.* This website, maintained by respected retirement researcher Wade Pfau, Ph.D., contains several articles and books on retirement income planning.

- The websites of Fidelity, Schwab, T. Rowe Price, and Vanguard all have many descriptive materials regarding the various types of annuities and investments. They can be a good place to get started learning about the different types of investment options.

Social Security resources

Books describing Social Security details

- *Get What's Yours: The Secrets to Maxing Out Your Social Security,* by Laurence J. Kotlikoff and Philip Moeller. Simon & Schuster, 2016.

- *Social Security for Dummies, 2017 Edition,* by Jonathan Peterson. John Wiley & Sons, Inc., 2017.

- *Social Security: The Inside Story, 2018 Silver Anniversary Edition,* by Andy Landis. Thinking Retirement, 2018.

Social Security Administration website

- www.ssa.gov contains a wealth of information on the various provisions and benefits of Social Security. It includes the following calculators to estimate your benefits:
  - o Your *my Social Security* account is the most precise, taking into account the wage history that is on record for you.
  - o *Quick Calculator* will provide estimated benefits based on salary input that you provide.

Websites, articles, and online calculators

Here I identify a number of helpful websites. It's not practical to provide the URL here, but you can find these sites by searching for the name.

- AARP's Social Security calculator
- *Covisum Social Security Timing*
- Edelman Financial Engines is a large advisory firm that maintains a good Social Security planner.
- Fidelity Investments Social Security calculator
- Forbes.com, articles in 2019 on Social Security sustainability:
  - o "A Bad Reason to Start Social Security Benefits Early"
  - o "There Aren't That Many Good Reasons to Start Social Security Very Early"

- *Managing Retirement Decisions*, a series of articles published by the Society of Actuaries:
  - o "Deciding When to Claim Social Security"
- *Maximize My Social Security*
- National Academy of Social Insurance, a website that contains many articles and videos to learn about Social Security
- *Open Social Security*, a free, online Social Security optimizer
- *Social Security Choices*
- *Social Security Solutions*

Acknowledgments

I'm very grateful to two people who helped me every step of the way, from brainstorming the initial concept to final production: my wife, Melinda, who applied her experience and expertise from her 30-year career in book publishing, and Teresa Ciulla, my talented editor. Melinda and Teresa read and edited the entire manuscript several times and spent countless hours brainstorming the issues we wanted to cover. Both helped me consider the layperson's perspective, and their efforts made *Don't Go Broke in Retirement* much easier to read and understand. I couldn't have written this book without them.

Teresa's husband, Jack Ciulla, read the entire manuscript from a layperson's perspective. He provided great comments that helped make the book more understandable and useful.

Marla Markman served as the project manager, helping bring the manuscript into its final form with her production services and expertise. Lisa Winger did a great job with designing the front and back covers, and designing the layout of the text. Our daughters Bonnie and Emily also helped with comments on the cover design. Thanks also to Allison Phillips and Wyn Hilty, who both proofread the entire manuscript and provided another review.

I'm very grateful for the opportunity to work at the Stanford Center on Longevity, where I conducted the research on retirement income strategies that's featured in this book.

In particular, I appreciate the input on these projects from Martha Deevy, associate director of the Center.

I've been very fortunate to work closely with Wade Pfau, Ph.D., and Joe Tomlinson, FSA, on these research projects. Joe reviewed the entire manuscript and provided invaluable comments on the technical accuracy as well as organization.

Anna Rappaport, FSA, also reviewed the entire manuscript and made many helpful suggestions. In addition, I'm deeply indebted to Steve Siegel and Barbara Scott at the Society of Actuaries for sponsoring much of the research on retirement income strategies that we conducted at the Stanford Center on Longevity.

Finally, over the years I've gained valuable insights from conversations with various experts in retirement income strategies, including Carol Bogosian, Toni Brown, Dirk Cotton, Mark Iwry, Andy Landis, Cindy Levering, Neil Lloyd, Bob Melia, Pete Neuwirth, Bob Powell, Allan Roth, Bill Sharpe, John Shoven, Ken Steiner, and Jack Towarnicky.

Don't Go Broke in Retirement wouldn't have been published without all of this help, so I'm very grateful to be part of such a wonderful community.

Index

P

payout rates, 35-37

pension plan, xii, xv, 6-7, 19, 59-60, 64-66, 68, 106, 108, 142, 144, 150, 159

period certain annuity, 63

R

real estate investment trusts (REIT), 49

required minimum distribution (RMD)

    alternative RIGs, 83-84, 87-90

    defined, 33, 35, 109, 150

    examples, 38-39, 77, 99, 112, 114, 120-121, 127-129, 133

    modifications, 83, 85-87, 142-143

    recent changes, 11, 33-34

    use in *Spend Safely Strategy*, 11-12, 16, 34, 43-44, 47, 65, 70, 75, 91, 93, 127, 140, 142, 144

    withdrawal percentages, 35-37

    work-arounds, 39-40,

retirement bonus, 7, 10-12, 16, 26, 30, 32-34, 38-40, 43-48, 50, 54-55, 59, 65, 70-73, 76-78, 80-81, 83-91, 93-94, 99-100, 111, 114, 116, 118, 120-122, 127-130, 133-137, 144-145

Retirement Game-Changers: Strategies for a Healthy, Financially Secure, and Fulfilling Long Life, xv, 8, 19, 24, 68, 75, 82

Retirement Income Generator (RIG), 4, 7, 10-11, 18, 28, 30, 42-43, 65, 83-86, 88, 90-91, 100, 112, 119

retirement income statements, 42-43

retirement paycheck, 6-8, 12, 16, 18, 24, 30, 34, 40, 45, 52-53, 59-60, 63, 65-66, 69, 73-74, 78-79, 94, 98, 101, 143-146

reverse mortgages, 59, 66-68, 74, 145

Roth 401(k), 107, 109

Roth IRA, 33, 75, 88, 107, 109

S

Schwab, 41, 51, 61

SECURE Act, 42-43

SEP-IRA, xii

sequence of returns risk, 31

About The Author

For more than 40 years, Steve Vernon, FSA, has analyzed, researched, and communicated about the most difficult retirement topics, including finances, health and lifestyle. He had a 30-year career as a consulting actuary with Watson Wyatt and Mercer, helping Fortune 1000 employers manage and communicate their retirement programs. During that time, he worked on the front lines of the extraordinary shift that's taken place in retirement plans, as employers switched from traditional, defined benefit pension plans to 401(k) and other defined contribution plans.

Steve has served for more than seven years in his encore career as a Research Scholar at the Stanford Center on Longevity. He's also president of *Rest-of-Life* Communications, a company he founded that delivers retirement planning workshops and conducts retirement education campaigns. He has never sold insurance, annuities, or investments; this enables him to be unbiased in his writing and recommendations.

His previously published works include:

- *Retirement Game-Changers: Strategies for a Healthy, Financially Secure, and Fulfilling Long Life. Rest-of-Life* Communications, 2018.

- *Recession-Proof Your Retirement Years: Simple Retirement Planning Strategies That Work Through Thick or Thin. Rest-of-Life* Communications, 2014.

- *Money for Life: Turn Your IRA and 401(k) Into a Lifetime Retirement Paycheck.* Rest-of-Life Communications, 2012.
- *The Quest: For Long Life, Health and Prosperity* (a DVD/workbook set). *Rest-of-Life* Communications, 2007.
- *Live Long & Prosper! Invest in Your Happiness, Health, and Wealth for Retirement and Beyond.* Wiley, 2005.
- *Don't Work Forever! Simple Steps Baby Boomers Must Take to <u>Ever</u> Retire.* Wiley, 1995.

Steve has published over 1,000 posts on retirement topics for CBS MoneyWatch, and he currently writes for Forbes.com.

A Fellow in the Society of Actuaries, Steve graduated summa cum laude from the University of California, Irvine, with a double major in mathematics and social science.

Steve lives in Oxnard, California, with his wife, Melinda, where they're following the advice in this book for their own retirement and rest-of-life. For more information, visit www.restoflife.com.